Keep On Onnin'

First published 2007 by order of the Tate Trustees
by Tate Britain

in association with
Tate Publishing, a division of Tate Enterprises Ltd,
Millbank, London SW1P 4RG
www.tate.org.uk/publishing

to document Art Now at Tate Britain 2004–7

© Tate 2007

British Library Cataloguing in Publication Data
A catalogue record for this book is available from
the British Library

ISBN 978 1 85437 770 8

Library of Congress Cataloguing in Publication Data
Library of Congress Control Number: 2007928193

Designed by Fraser Muggeridge studio
Printing co-ordinated by Uwe Kraus

Front & back cover: Joanne Tatham & Tom O'Sullivan,
Think, Think Thingamajig; what do you represent? 2006,
performance at Tate Britain
Courtesy the artists

Keep On Onnin'

Contemporary Art at Tate Britain
Art Now 2004–7

Contents

Art Now space

Sculpture Court

Lightbox

Live

Foreword

The Art Now programme at Tate Britain quickens the pace at which contemporary art moves from the intimate space of the studio to the public space of the gallery. It provides a vital platform for artists in the early stages of their career, and opens up public discussion of their imaginative and material preoccupations. This encounter between the artwork and the audience can be a chance affair, at times unpredictable and untraceable. Unlike much of what is shown elsewhere in the building, this art has not had time to settle. There is, inevitably, an air of uncertainty at this moment of exposure. And it is in that 'unsettling' moment that viewers can discover something entirely new.

This important series responds to developments in contemporary practice, and is a core part of Tate Britain's involvement in contemporary art, which also includes displays of recent acquisitions, the Turner Prize, an annual Duveens Commission, the Tate Triennial, as well as major survey shows. From summer 2007 the Art Now exhibitions will be even more visible, as they are relocated to the very centre of the building. The programme colonises other gallery spaces too, with commissioned work shown outdoors, and regular film and video programmes in the Lightbox space. Live and performance work is also presented, and all these different manifestations together create a complex web of ideas, attitudes and positions.

This book collects together over thirty individual artists' presentations. A number of Tate curators have invested huge energy and commitment in the research and programming of this series, notably Lizzie Carey-Thomas, Katharine Stout, and Rachel Tant, who have also edited this publication. They have been joined at different stages by Gair Boase, Emily Pethick, Ben Tufnell and Catherine Wood – all of whom have made important contributions to the development and success of the programme.

Art Now relies on the professionalism and dedication of many others too. The Tate Britain team has greatly enjoyed our collaboration with Film and Video Umbrella, and in particular Stephen Bode and Caroline Smith. At Tate, thanks are due to Christina Bagatavicius, Jennifer Batchelor, Helen Beeckmans, Kieran Begley, Louise Butler, Gillian Buttimer, Mikei Hall, Hayley James, Gemma Nightingale, Kiko Noda, Philip Miles, Shuja Rahman, Louise Ramsay, Adrian Shaw, Andy Shiel, Liam Tebbs, Tate Art Handling, Tate Conservation and Tate Photography.

Fraser Muggeridge and Sven Herzog have given this publication its elegant design, and Judith Van Ingen brought great dedication to its production. Our thanks to those who took part in the discussion: Jananne Al-Ani, Kate Davis, Andrew Grassie, Sally O'Reilly and Ian White, with Lizzie Carey-Thomas and Katharine Stout. Above all, we extend huge thanks and appreciation to all the artists for taking the opportunity to show their work in this particular context at Tate Britain.

Judith Nesbitt, Chief Curator

JA   Jananne Al-Ani, *artist*
LCT   Lizzie Carey-Thomas, *Tate curator*
KD   Kate Davis, *artist*
AG   Andrew Grassie, *artist*
SOR Sally O'Reilly, *writer and critic*
KS   Katharine Stout, *Tate curator*
IW   Ian White, *artist and curator*

Art Now panel discussion

LCT Let me first give some background to the Art Now programme. It was set up in 1995, specifically as a platform to show work by younger artists at the Tate Gallery. At that point Tate's commitment to contemporary art was largely fulfilled by the Turner Prize which had been running for eleven years. Artists selected for the new Art Now space included Matthew Barney, Sophie Calle and Mark Dion, so many of them were already well established on the international scene. When the Tate divided into Tate Modern and Tate Britain in 2000 the remit was adjusted so that the artists being represented were British or British based. Art Now has continually aimed to reflect current practice, at a faster pace than the rest of the programme. In 2003, we introduced the Lightbox film and video programme and more recently have incorporated live art. In June Art Now will relocate to a new space, which is almost double the size, at the centre of the gallery. In the previous Art Now publication, the writer Martin Herbert described the programme as operating like a 'micro-kunsthalle' within the institution… So Art Now offers artists a public platform as opposed to a commercial context; a broad and large audience that artists might not necessarily have access to at that point in their careers; the support of a public institution, and in Tate Britain's case, the context of a historical collection. Against the backdrop of the rapid growth of the contemporary art market and the plethora of new spaces both public and private, I'd like to ask your views on how Art Now relates to all of this?

IW One thing that strikes me is that it seems to be quite tied to the market. That it is not, in fact, especially separate. I think the Art Now programme generally reflects an art market.

SOR I think you're right in saying that the programme does reflect an art market, but hopefully what Art Now can do is provide a space where an artist could do something that the art market would find difficult to swallow, whether in its contentiousness or just its form. For instance, I think bringing live art into the actual structure of the programme, rather than it being an auxiliary or just associated with the artists who are showing in the space, is something that generally doesn't happen in commercial galleries.

KD I'd agree with that, and I think that it is crucial, in terms of giving artists a context that isn't a commercial gallery, and the freedom to be ambitious within another remit. It locates your work in a particular and significant history, and that placement undoubtedly holds wider repercussions for an artist's practice. In this way, Art Now could be more relevant to an artist's aims and practice, rather than placing commerical concerns or restraints on artistic production.

Tate Britain, exterior
Courtesy Tate

IW   I still don't show work commercially at all. But I don't think I'm typical in this. The work I made for Art Now was in collaboration with Jimmy Robert and he has since shown with a commercial gallery. Do you think that the works that are shown in this space are entirely outside of the market? That they don't ever enter back into the market, or they don't come from the market? Because I don't think that's the case. I think that they are part of it.

SOR   I don't think that it is a different voice at all. I think it is the same vocabulary spoken in the same voices, just maybe they're saying slightly longer words. That's a terrible analogy!

AG   I think that it's a slight inflection on the same conversation. It can be seen as a really good career move to be shown in a museum. As far as a commercial gallery goes, I know they look for artists who have museum shows behind them, and in that sense it is important to tick off the boxes. But it was also just a great opportunity for me, as I tend to work within quite a strict brief and a specific location. Tate was my fantasy space to show in, having grown up visiting it with my parents.

LCT   Kate, you addressed the context of Tate Britain when showing your work too. You made a very personal response to Epstein's *Rockdrill* and also the work of Barbara Kruger. How important was it to conceive your project especially for the Art Now space, and within the context of the collection?

KD   I've been interested in making work that is related to the context of the exhibition; the ideas often begin with the site. Tate Britain offers such a rich source in that regard. It felt exciting to be able to think about the collection and to respond to that. I suppose it is a site that, as someone interested in art and being an artist, you continually revisit, so we have our own memories of the exhibitions that we've seen here. Art Now provided an opportunity and a responsibility to do something that I felt strongly about in relation to that location.

KS   And Ian, you directly engaged the institution when you and Jimmy Robert selected a work from the collection to be hung during your performance.

IW   I don't think that part of the performance was initially conceived as being as much of an institutional critique as it became. One of the things that we wanted to explore was the idea of hanging paintings as part of the performance and it was initially a very simple idea. But it didn't take very long to find out that this can cause huge problems and so we ended up with Tate art handlers hanging and unhanging the work whilst Jimmy and I were performing. I suppose what we got from that, in a project that was very process-based, was a sense of finding our weight. Not in terms of our status within the institution, but finding a way through institutions as part of the process of making the piece. I suppose I would challenge this idea that the space is about freedom. I think we encountered a lot of restriction, and built that into the project. There were strange frames put around the work that we wouldn't have chosen. The way the work was described on the wall label was peculiar and didn't really relate to what we were doing or how we wanted to articulate ourselves. That's just one example, but we tried to embody these things within the work, rather than mask them.

LCT   We've noticed an increasing self-awareness about the context of the institution when artists are invited to exhibit here. Enrico David's sculpture court commission drew attention to the sculpture court as a physical annex or offshoot of the museum but also as a social space, and at the same time conformed to the conventions of a sculpture court, by presenting an autonomous work there. Raqib Shaw made work in response to the Holbein exhibition which was showing at the same time, and Rory Macbeth led fantasy tours around the collection, as part of the live event last December.

KS   I think if you try to work differently within an institution like the Tate, you immediately encounter its structure and constraints, other considerations that may not arise in other places.

JA   Almost all of my work has been shown in publicly funded spaces. The difference with the Tate is that it's also a tourist attraction, not just an art gallery, so there seems to be a very different relationship between the audience and the work. Compared to a commercial gallery or a smaller public art gallery, it definitely attracts a different kind of audience. My guess would be that a large percentage of the audience was not interested in my work at all but had come to see the historic collection. Also, although huge numbers move through the Art Now exhibitions there's actually no mechanism for you to get any sense of their response.

JA   It definitely felt as if the Art Now room was a space that people happened upon.

LCT   Do you think that had its merits?

IW   I suppose it is a shame it feels a bit like a cupboard at the back of the museum, but at the same time, so be it.

JA   I think each of us worked our way into that space in different ways. Personally, I wasn't invited to make work in response to the space. Film and Video Umbrella, who originally commissioned the work, approached different venues to host the show. It was a very different relationship from the usual approach, to make something site-specific. How does it normally work?

KS   There is no set way. What we try to do is offer a platform for showing artists at a certain stage of their careers. We use the term 'emerging', which essentially means artists in the first decade of establishing their practice. We encourage new work to be made, not necessarily commissioning, but hopefully enabling artists to realise a new work already conceived of. I think the question of whether Art Now offers a unique situation is really interesting. Also, at what stage of an artist's career is institutional validation a good thing? Commercial galleries occasionally approach us, and I think you have to acknowledge that an artist with support can often be made more visible. Is it possible, given the growing strength of the market, to make judgements independent of it?

SOR   It is becoming increasingly difficult to do anything independently. Somehow as the market absorbs more and more practices, the grass-roots way of getting your hands dirty and scrabbling for a living doesn't seem to be happening so much. There is a bit of a problem with the idea of an institution like this absorbing people from the commercial sector, validating a self-perpetuating, snowballing effect of commercialisation. I'm always trying to find ways of circumventing this. You can only ever reach a certain level of production, I think, trying to operate independently. It is a problem at the moment.

LCT   We have an obligation to try to do something about that, by actively seeking out artists who aren't represented.

SOR   Of course. It is just about finding a parallel route for artists, which isn't through the commercial sector.

IW   I'm starting to think that these two things are actually connected. The Tate as an institution has expanded exponentially, and not just in terms of the volume of space it occupies, but the different registers of space that it tries to occupy. Art Now is a very good example of Tate wanting to occupy a small, more dynamic space, whilst also having major retrospective exhibitions, or historical survey shows, and doing these things simultaneously. This perhaps finds a parallel in the way the commercial gallery sector finds it easier to absorb a range of different practices, as Sally was just describing, whereby performance work or the more ephemeral practices can actually be sold.

KS   So sometimes a commercial gallery, depending on its ethos, can also be a free space?

IW   In a sense, yes. I think it is interesting to know what your curatorial processes are. Your account of the Art Now space seems to be both within the institution but also outside it, and outside the commercial system but also within it. I think one way it becomes different is if you have a different curatorial process from other institutional processes.

LCT   Maybe we should say a bit about how we put the programme together. The programme has three curators dedicated to it. We do a lot of studio visits and research, keeping up to date with artists we're interested in, and are constantly looking out for others. Generally we have a lot of freedom. We're trying to reflect what is going on in current practice but there isn't a template for how we do that, and we're also mindful of trying to get a balance of media and different approaches to making work, but without fulfilling any strict criteria. Decisions are made through a process of discussion between the three curators. Occasionally we get approached by other organisations, and if there is a project they bring to our attention that we think is really worth supporting then, like Jananne's, we will take that opportunity. Primarily we're proactive in approaching artists and asking them whether they'd like to take part. So it is quite a free-form thing, and because of that, and because it doesn't go through many layers of approval within the institution, it operates at a different pace from other aspects of the gallery's programme.

KS   But at the same time, I don't think we're proposing that it's a radical process within the institution. For me, it comes back to the question of at what stage in an artist's career we should be showing artists in Art Now. I think it's natural the institution should validate artists who are already coming to the attention of other curators, other spaces, whether commercial or public, since we are part of that network. I don't think it's appropriate for us to be curating very new talent, for example an artist straight out of college who seems to be the next hot thing. Often it will be an artist's first solo show in an institution and I see our curatorial role as helping them with that context, with the different language that we need to use, not just for an audience that is critically engaged but also for a tourist who has just stepped off the plane from Japan. As you say, Ian, the Tate is ever-expanding. Are we stepping on other people's toes?

KD   I think there's a real need for a space like Art Now, as the commercial scene in Britain continues to grow. It's not operating independently of that market, but possibly the selection of work can be independent of those concerns. So whether it's Rory Macbeth doing his guided tour or Sue Tompkins doing a live performance, or an exhibition of Michael Fullerton's work, it seems that we need to be able to view work on its own merits. It's essential that there is the space to be able to pursue a more serious inquiry into the work itself.

AG   Public space is free. You will get the tourists and all the rest of it, which is a huge plus. But do you feel you might be duplicating what other spaces are doing? Do you feel any signs of antagonism?

KS   No, I don't think so, because the appetite for contemporary art has increased. But when we programme we are aware of which artists are showing in the network of publicly funded galleries, such as Chisenhale Gallery or Camden Arts Centre, as well as commercial galleries. But hopefully there's not a conflict, in the sense that there are so many interesting artists to show.

SOR   One thing that Art Now could do is commission more ambitious projects, such as big films, that aren't necessarily supported elsewhere.

IW   As the co-ordinator of The Artists Cinema at Frieze Art Fair in 2005 and 2006 have to contest that! Each year, Frieze Projects and LUX commissioned five artists to make new work, shown in cinemas all over the country and internationally.

JA   The problem is being able to watch them in that mad context.

KS   Frieze offers not only the commercial context but also commissioning opportunities. In a sense, it offers everything, and raises the question of what other spaces can offer that is distinctive. Perhaps the ability to spend time in a contemplative space? Is that what an institution can offer?

JA   I don't know about your funding structure, but what kind of projects would you be able to commission?

LCT   We have one budget for the year so we try to allocate each project broadly the same amount of money. We offer a small fee to each artist, and we can help with fabrication, but we don't attempt to commission work as our budget couldn't support this. However, we do collaborate with organisations like Film and Video Umbrella. Commercial galleries are now able to offer production budgets or possibilities in a much greater way than public-funded institutions, whereas here budgets are continually scrutinised and under pressure. The market is obviously in everyone's minds at the moment, so I wondered if you think its growing success is generally a positive thing?

KS   Let's put Kate on the spot and ask her to talk about being based in Glasgow, and her involvement in Transmission, which is essentially a non-profit artist-run gallery. Certainly in London it is very hard for artist-run spaces to be sustainable.

KD   I think Glasgow is in quite an unusual position at the moment. It feels as if it is in the middle of substantial change and that is to do with the fact that really, for the last ten years or so, the main alternative spaces were Modern Institute and Transmission and the public institutions, the CCA and Tramway. But in the last few years other commercial spaces have emerged

Transmission Gallery, Glasgow
Transmission Gallery

like Sorcha Dallas and Mary Mary and this has had an effect. Modern Institute has been crucial in giving artists the motivation to remain living in the city, rather than take their work somewhere else. It has been really encouraging for the younger generation to see more established artists like Christine Borland or Cathy Wilkes, even Douglas Gordon, who have at least partially stayed within the city. Transmission has given artists the opportunity to participate in an active art scene. Funded by the Scottish Arts Council and run by a rolling committee of six artists, Transmission has the freedom (in the most part) to curate work that the gallery thinks is important within a budget that means you could invite an artist from Dundee to show alongside someone from New York. It is important to be giving that work exposure in a Scottish gallery which anyone can become a member of. I suppose it just feels as though the market is starting to have an effect on Glasgow, and I just hope that the art community doesn't lose some of the priorities that a space like Transmission embodies.

LCT　There is an assumption that Glasgow offers a space that is slightly outside of market constraints, and artists can go about the studio practice without feeling under pressure to produce work that will sell. Do you think that's the case?

KD　I think that there is a healthy critical discourse within the art community which, in the past, has been largely removed from a dominant commercial voice. It is interesting to see how the success of particular artists in Scotland has infiltrated some of the art schools, and slightly altered the mentality of students, maybe giving them more ambition towards the possibility of making money from work.

LCT　Ian, you teach as well, is this your experience?

IW　I didn't go to art school, so I don't really have a sense of how it was before now. Most of the teaching I've done has been in the past three or four years and I think the awareness of the commercial sector in the art school is extraordinary. I find that really fascinating. At the same time I also don't think it is inaccurate to try to explain what the commercial system is. I think that if you choose to try to earn your money as an artist by making work and selling it, then that functions in a very particular way. And I think part of that is about participating in a private-view circuit, which some art schools would encourage. The question for students is, 'How do I get shown in a commercial gallery?' Well, one way is to hang out in the right private views, and do that for as many times as it takes to get a show. I really do think that's how, in part, the commercial circuit in London in particular functions. Of course, the other answer is to make 'good' work. At the moment I choose not to participate in terms of trying to sell work though this might change.

KS　There's a slight undertone in this conversation that commercial is a dirty word.

AG   Well I positively encourage my students to get involved in the commercial
      art scene. Just to see it for what it is. I just wish they would go to more
      galleries and get a sense of the cog-wheels of the art world. They can then
      respond to it however they want, critically or however they choose, but not
      to be aware of it seems to me that you're just cutting down the opportunity
      to speak.

JA   I think it is good that they understand the realities of the commerical sector
      or most of them are going to be sorely disappointed when they realise
      they're not going to be represented by White Cube.

SOR   There's a massive upsurge in this thing called professional practice in art
      schools, and I don't think that's a bad thing. It depends on how it is taught,
      but it is really important that they understand the context in which they
      will be judged. Every aspect of it.

KS   Sally, from the perspective of a writer and critic, what do you think about
      the growth of the market and the dominance of it at the moment?

SOR   I have some ambivalence towards the market, and this does tie in with
      teaching and also with writing, but for me the important thing is to focus
      absolutely on the work. I'm hardly ever in the same room as collectors.
      I exist in a parallel realm to the money in the art world, and I don't think
      collectors are reading my reviews and making decisions based upon that
      at all. Maybe my ambivalence comes from considering a market that
      is so overwhelming, as in New York, where any sense of criticality seems
      irrelevant. I find it extremely depressing, this other way of thinking about
      work entirely, which is not to do with ideology, or artists' intentions,
      or interpretation, or any of those things. I don't think we're there yet in
      Britain, and even colleges that do groom students for commercial success
      still absolutely emphasise the critical understanding of art and art history
      and critical theory. So it is an okay balance right now, and of course artists
      have to survive and I obviously accept the fact that I write for money as well.

LCT   And how does an artist respond to art fairs? Certainly Frieze has had quite
      an effect on the London art world, with museums and galleries aligning
      their autumn programmes with the events of Frieze week. So how do
      you position yourself in relation to that? Is it a context that you can use
      in a productive way? Or is it something that you simply accept as part
      of the deal?

IW   I find it fascinating, this perception that Frieze Art Fair represents some
      other realm. I don't think it does. I think that the art fair and the museum
      are indivisible from each other.

KS   Obviously they're completely different viewing experiences?

Frieze Art Fair, London 2006
Photography: Linda Nylind

IW But I think that's a mask. To treat it on that level is inaccurate. I think that museums are entirely oriented around the art fair happening at a particular point in the year. I think that they share an engagement with a kind of entertainment culture that is reflected for example by live performance programmes throughout the year.

SOR Why does live performance reflect entertainment more than a room full of paintings?

IW I think that's a really good question. I think the idea of a space like Art Now is connected to a pervasive entertainment culture, and again I don't necessarily think that's a bad thing. I do question it, obviously.

SOR There is an idea that entertainment is a bad thing, but actually it is simply another way of operating.

KS That's something that I was thinking about at the beginning of the discussion, when we were talking about footfall and the difference between showing at the Tate and other spaces. The sheer volume of people who now visit Tate Modern in particular is extraordinary. How much resistance is there to the idea of art as entertainment? What capacity do artists have to resist that? Is it a problem that contemporary art is now so popular? Is this related to the rising interest in live art, in terms of it being a different kind of experience, one that the performer is perhaps more in control of?

SOR I think art, like food, is consumed in different ways, at different rates and for different reasons. An artist whose work is appreciated by the wider public is maybe very lucky, but may not be accepted on a critical level by art world specialists. Not that it is one or the other.

JA What about works that don't appeal to the masses? Do you think they will then be less likely to get shown?

SOR I think that the people who programme these spaces have half an eye on the general acceptance or reading of these things, but are still also aware of critical debates and discussions. I hope so!

KS Something else we wanted to touch upon is the criterion that artists are based in Britain, or British born and living elsewhere. What does that mean to you as artists? How important is nationality? Is it more about locality, *where* people are making art?

SOR In London in particular there is such an international flux.

KS That's why in a way it doesn't seem too restrictive, because at least half the artists that we show didn't grow up in Britain. Why is London such a draw?

IW   I think the danger is conflating London with the UK. It is incredibly regionalist. My experience of the London art scene is that I think it's very prejudiced, actually, and artists working outside of London showing at Tate are received very differently.

KS   In terms of programming, we try to get a balance between keeping up with what's happening in London and visiting studios and exhibitions elsewhere. But because London is such a strong magnet, artists end up relocating here as well.

SOR We are lucky here in having such an international flow of people coming through London that our gaze is naturally pulled outwards by the people who come and go; it doesn't feel so much of a problem.

AG   Personally, I moved to London from Edinburgh as soon as I could buy a train ticket, to do my art foundation, but I don't want to be prejudiced. I think as long as people aren't blinkered and look outside of London, there really isn't a problem. Then again, I didn't actually show here for seven years after leaving art college. I didn't know where to look. But as the market rose in the mid-1990s so too did a number of artist-run galleries in the East End. You could show there and have an audience of fifty or sixty people, then slowly you could step up to greater opportunities. That's very important, to have this sort of 'ladder' to climb. For me, my Art Now exhibition was a different experience from showing in a commercial gallery and was another step on the 'ladder'.

LCT Do you feel that you could be based anywhere else?

AG   I honestly feel that I couldn't. My fear is that I would just dissolve. That's probably not true and rational, but that's why I'm here. I spent years wanting to leave London but thinking I couldn't possibly. Most of my work is about the actual practice of making work. I fear that if I were isolated there would simply be less to respond to, fewer opportunities to interact with the stuff that makes up art.

KD   I think there are benefits to not living in London, especially in terms of quality of life. I need that to be able to work; to have my studio and have a structure of people around me who can help me make work; where close relationships are quite easy and support is accessible. I find that really helpful. I feel the opposite way about London. I get stimulated by coming to London when I need to. Then I have to recover to be able to make work. Not that I don't thrive on stress as well!

SOR   With any conglomeration of practitioners, which can happen in any density of population in a city or town, it's the critical network and the discussions that are important.

LCT   I guess there's a constant mirror to what you're doing.

IW   I don't think it is so much about being British or living in London. It is certainly about being validated by the institution.

JA   You are validated by the institution, like it or not. It affects the way people see you as an artist. The Tate is now an international brand. If I go to the Middle East and say I'm having a show at the Tate, people know what I'm talking about.

KS   Something else we wanted to touch upon is live art. Looking back over the last few years, do you think live and performance art has come to the forefront of contemporary practice?

SOR   The impetus behind organising live things is one of risk and delight. There does seem to be more consideration of this recently as a viable practice. Although it still tends to be seen as an auxiliary thing, it is becoming more central. Some artists, like Lali Chetwynd and Pil and Galia Kollectiv, will also show the props or the costumes which are then sold as an artwork. However, I think increasingly people are being encouraged to do performance work for no other reason than that it is seen as a valid mode of production.

LCT   This connects to looking at how artists are increasingly moving more fluidly between the roles of curator or producer and taking control of framing and presenting their work, as well as making it. Is that about trying to gain control within the system; not only in the way that work is produced but also how it is perceived?

JA   One of the reasons I started curating shows was absolutely to have control over the context in which my work was being seen. Most artists are sensitive about this but it's often more strongly felt by those who are identified by their difference in some way. In recent years I've been approached by a number of curators with crude proposals for shows about the Middle East or Arab or Muslim artists, with no real curatorial narrative. So, curating is a way of taking charge of that… and all the stuff you were referring to Lizzie: being in control of what gets written for the labels, how the catalogue is produced and all the other things that contextualise your work. But I'm not sure it is an effective strategy. I tried it, and I'm not sure… it is a lot of effort for a small return.

SOR I know some performance artists who until recently felt extremely marginalised. They feel as though they're rolled in as entertainment, and are extremely badly paid.

KS So you think live art is more prevalent in contemporary practice simply because institutions recognise it more, rather than it being a growing interest for artists who choose to work in that way?

SOR I think it's a snowballing effect of validation.

LCT Ian, I found your performance really moving. There was an awareness of you and Jimmy going through a process that put you on a spot. The viewer didn't quite know what might happen. It was difficult and very concentrated, in a very public way. In a sense, performance art reveals all of that. Obviously having an exhibition is similar, but the artist is removed from the equation in time and space.

SOR A lot of artists think performance is about spontaneity and improvisation, but rehearsal and ability and skills are starting to figure a bit more as well.

IW Our performance explored the body as an agency. Rather than revealing something about our lives, we were interested in something more abstract, which was about the passing of time. Or, how do you work over time and enable that to inform something that people watch? But it wasn't confessional in that sense. It was absolutely about that moment and being in that moment with an audience.

LCT But you and Jimmy had a display in the Art Now space, a residue of the performance, how did you see that working?

IW I think people found the work we showed in the Art Now space quite difficult to interpret. And maybe it was. The thing in common between all of the works in that space was the passing of time; how to mark the passing of time, and so in a way that was the unifying theme.

LCT As an aside, it is interesting that all of your works actually dealt with the passing of time in some way. Andrew, yours was showing the evidence of something that had once been in the space and wasn't any more, so created a sense of being in two spaces simultaneously: the Art Now space with your work presented in it, and the Art Now space as it had been with the Tate Collection works you brought together. And Kate, you were engaged with art from the past and bringing it back into the present.

KD Maybe it has something to do with the prevalence of the history of the institution? I think that we are continually confronted with moments in time. I always feel I am looking at things and trying to situate them within the context of when they were made. For me, being given the chance to make work for the Tate, I was trying to locate myself and what I'm doing within that history. So I suppose time is really critical to that.

JA The history of the Tate interests me. I think the history of British cultural institutions in general is fascinating and very often problematic. I'd much rather show here than in Tate Modern, which doesn't have the narrative of the institution embedded in it in quite the same way.

KS It does seem that artists particularly want to respond to the context of Tate Britain. What I think is interesting is that this is the building many artists grew up with in terms of coming to see art, so it will be interesting to see what happens with the generation who also visit Tate Modern. But for us the history is what remains interesting and pertinent. Artists seem to be interested in revisiting history or using work by other artists as a starting point. That seems to fit very well with the context here.

AG I wonder how much Art Now will change, when it moves to a more centralised space?

LCT There is still uncertainty about whether Tate Britain only shows historic art. One of the motivations for moving the Art Now gallery to the heart of Tate Britain is to assert our commitment to contemporary art.

AG In a way, you're a necessary 'other' within the institution itself. As a space for unknown artists – as perceived by the audience who comes here – it's almost a radical, inherent core, which maintains the bigger structure. So in a sense, by relocating Art Now more centrally, it recognises its role to the overall structure.

March 2007

Art Now space

Unless otherwise stated 'installation views' refers to the Art Now space

The Colonist 2004, installation view, Meyer Riegger, Karlsruhe
Courtesy the artist, Maureen Paley, London, and Meyer Riegger, Karlsruhe

David Thorpe
The Colonist

David Thorpe's body of work to date considers the extent to which pictures, and more recently sculptural objects, offer pathways to new orders of experience. Thorpe considers this constructed 'world' of the art object as an ambiguously privileged and paranoid domain.

The artist's earliest work in the mid-late 1990s derived from a fascination with film images. In cutting and pasting coloured sugar paper to make his own pictures, resembling simplified film stills, the artist discovered a method of claiming the promise that such widely-consumed images offered: of building a tangible link between their imaginary world and his existence in real time. These collages conflated romantic cityscapes drawn from American and European films with fantastical projections of the architectural skyline of south-east London where he lived, blending local and pop cultural referents.

By forging such links between imagined and 'found' imagery, Thorpe began to explore the meeting point between individual agency and the world as a given. Works from 1997 depict large-scale structures which propose the possibility of enjoyment; some by creative ingenuity on the part of the participants, some by design. Silhouetted nightscapes of people at funfairs and in cable cars appeared alongside compositions of ordinary architectural structures reclaimed by city inhabitants: pylons imagined as gigantic climbing frames in *Fun*, or a motorway flyover as viewing spot for a shooting star in *Need for Speed*.

The Colonist 2004
Courtesy the Goetz Collection, Munich

In the late 1990s, Thorpe's engagement with his materials began to take on greater complexity, moving towards the dense layering of the current work. Image sources shifted from the city towards grand wildernesses with curious architectural structures set within them. In works such as *Out from the Night the Day is Beautiful …*, 1999,

showing a hang-glider set against soaring pines in a mountain landscape,
the increasingly complex arrangement of tiny pieces creates a contoured surface
with a resemblance to camouflage.

This thickening of surface in the collages pointed to the moment at which
Thorpe's practice began, productively, to turn in on itself. The work began by
reaching towards an existing, but otherwise unobtainable, image world, but
after this point the artist's manipulation of materials had begun to offer endless
possibilities of invention itself. Recent collages incorporate all manner of found
matter, from tissue paper through to dried bark, mass-produced jewellery, slate,
glass and dried grasses and flowers. Yet the current installation, *The Colonist*,
demonstrates the extent to which the artist's world has expanded from the image
world to include the gallery space in four dimensions. Elements of sculpture
and architecture are now integral to the work.

Installed together, the objects and pictures in this exhibition set up complex
chains of connection. The sculptures on display double as practical objects which
might feature in the world of Thorpe's images, and as simple aesthetic objects.
Resembling a rudimentary weapon, the missile-like shape of *Eternity and
Resistance* echoes an earlier collage of a rocket-like habitation. The bow structure
of *The Axe Cuts the Root* matches the shallow curve of the dam in *The Axe Laid
on the Root*. Other works are akin to provisional models for housing. *The White
Brotherhood* is designed as a miniature 'lean-to' containing moveable dowel pieces
with the potential for sparking fire. Continuous shifts in scale, from a house
pictured in a collage to an abstract architectural model, to a large-scale screen,
frustrate the possibility of concrete moments of representational realism. Thorpe's
watercolours appear to offer some truth as 'pure' specimens of the natural biology
of the world from his vision. But studied closely, these plants themselves are
shot through with the geometries of man-made culture. This world is built upon
a foundation of human invention and endeavour.

In recent writing, Thorpe imagined the making of art in terms of military
defence strategy. In his work, it is not only the constructions of weapons and
fortress-like dwellings which place an emphasis on barriers, but also the literal
division and separation of gallery spaces by his wood and glass screens titled
The Protecting Army I–V. Thorpe's position in the studio is wilfully isolationist;
his own work and the work of others serving as the lifelines of communication
and sustenance. His elected 'advisors' are books and records by other artists,
musicians and architects. Sources range from the English Arts and Crafts
movement, particularly in the work of William Morris, to the musical cult
of Sun Ra and the writings on self-sufficient communalism by C.R. Ashbee.

Thorpe's work imagines a cultivated and defended 'new world' but he does
not work in the tradition of twentieth-century avant-gardism as a revolutionary
artist blazing the trail. His work operates with a different level of persuasion,
a kind of romantic appeal which points to the possibility of the existence of
a pocket of space for building one's own system of living, one's own freedom,

Opposite: *The White Brotherhood* 2004
Courtesy the artist, Maureen Paley, London, and Meyer Riegger, Karlsruhe

within an alienating and dysfunctional outside world. In this sense, the work balances carefully on a knife-edge of creativity and conservatism. The work foregrounds a sense of joy in labour as a kind of transformative process. But Thorpe acknowledges the artist-labourer's position as a luxurious – and therefore necessarily protected, and slightly paranoid – one.

Thorpe's configuration of images and objects offers a kind of fellowship to those who are open to engage with it, what he has termed a 'confederacy of seekers' who wish for such allegiance within a network of historical and current ideas. A performance which Thorpe staged at Tate Britain in 2003, *The Mighty Lights Community Project*, evoked a similar mood, proposing an imaginary 'meeting' of inhabitants of his world. Participants sung hymns and chants on the ambiguously enthusiastic and sinister theme of utopian communal living and belief in a shared, glorious future. The image of community in this work goes against the grain of contemporary notions of 'participatory' practice with democratic appeal, implying a certain elitism. Similarly, Thorpe's work extends a double-edged invitation and warding-off of communality, akin to Sun Ra's conception of his own philosophy offering 'a bridge to some, a wall to others'.

Catherine Wood

The Colonist 2004, installation views
Courtesy the artist, Maureen Paley, London, and Meyer Riegger, Karlsruhe

David Thorpe 33

6 Things we couldn't do, but can do now 2004, installation view
Courtesy the artists

Jimmy Robert & Ian White
6 things we couldn't do, but can do now

Jimmy Robert makes super-8 films in which the performance or re-staging
of minimal, everyday actions are shown to be exotic and tender at the same time.
Robert's performances combine social commentary with lyrical expression.
Ian White is a curator of artists' film and video and a writer, as well as a creator
of multi-format work that utilises slide, video, text and sound, in the form of events.

6 things… was Robert and White's first collaboration as artists. This project
consisted of a live performance (made twice) and a related installation including
drawings, paintings, objects and a video recording of American post-modern
choreographer Yvonne Rainer's seminal dance work *Trio A* 1965–6 (recorded
by Sally Banes in 1978). The performance work which paralleled the Art Now
installation proposed a minimalist-style grid of objects, with and against which
actions were carried out. In one action, wearing blue jeans and white T-shirts
with the Labour Party logo on, Robert stood on bricks as though on *pointe* shoes,
supported by White; in another a blank parade banner was carried diagonally
across the space as though miming a processional protest. *Trio A* was danced
in unison by the two artists, with the Rainer film on a monitor placed on the floor;
simultaneously Gil Leung and Simon Noble, two of Tate's art-handling team,
installed and de-installed a 1984 John Cage drawing according to exacting Tate
procedures on the back wall of the performance space. The actions performed by
White and Robert were introduced by the handing out of a programme sheet that
substituted the usual clarity of Tate-style interpretation with personal or anecdotal
information which the audience read at the start of the piece while the artists
sat on two chairs. The two elements of the project presented an ongoing process
that explored art-making and the possibility of exchange, making human relations
manifest. None of the works installed in the Art Now space were attributed to
either Robert or White exclusively, although some were made separately and some
together: all were made, or presented, as a result of the collaborative process.

The one hour performance took place on Saturday 20 November in the Manton
Foyer, Tate Britain and on Friday 3 December in Gallery 9, Tate Britain.

Catherine Wood

Catherine Wood: How and why did you come to work together on this project?

Jimmy Robert & Ian White: It was as naïve as us going to see Michael Clark perform at the Barbican last year. We both left with a similar idea; that it would be great to work on a performance together. The idea came from watching the dancers walk and run around the stage. We were thinking about the way their arms moved or didn't move and thinking about how we might come to make a piece where the process was foregrounded and non-spectacular: a process that could be a day trip to Hastings as much as time in a studio. That was on my [Jimmy's] birthday.

Are the exhibited or performed 'art object' and the collaborative process identical in this piece of work?

Is this piece of work identical to the process through which it was made? Yes and no. There is no sense of an ending in the work, just a continuous exchange. In the same way, there are no objects. The performance and the objects (drawings, paintings, prints) in the gallery all derive from a particular way of working, but so do most things that people make.

When we were working together, mainly in Amsterdam where Jimmy lives right now, we thought a lot about what constitutes work; what might constitute a process that was as much about coming to know each other as it was about finding a way of physically working together. We were coming from very different positions and needing to feel comfortable with each other to make things in ways we hadn't done before.

The performance and the exhibition represent repeated attempts to do this, in very different forms, but we do not consider either form to be definitive, quite distinct from the way that art objects often feel fixed and finished.

Is there an equivalence between your use of drawing and your use of choreographed movement in the work?

Maybe everything is drawing? There are actual pencil drawings, typewritten text (the automated mark) and then there is also the section in the performance where we physically move each other using pieces of A4 office paper, crumpling each sheet and making a physical impression. There is a relationship between gesture and mark-making. An equivalence maybe, but they are not illustrative of each other. We thought about the relationship between a plan and an elevation in architecture – a virtual three-dimensional model and its map. For example, in *Phrase*, the print on the gallery wall, the gesture of cutting and threading disrupts representation.

Choreography we understand as different from movement. This piece of work oscillates between the repeatable action (characteristic of choreography) and movements that are not planned, not strictly repeatable or prescribed. In that sense both the exploration of drawing and the different registers of movement in the performance (random, unintended, choreographed) are perhaps equivalent in their indeterminacy.

How do the presence of the art historical referents you have selected – the Yvonne Rainer piece, the Tate collection work – connect with your own work?

While both these things are connected by their historical status, we actually understand them separately. Learning Yvonne Rainer's *Trio A* was a very different thing from negotiating with the Tate to hang a work from their/your collection. I [Ian] work mainly as a curator, and I'm interested in the way in which interpretation (always present or mediated for us by the institution or curator when we view a work of art) can be re-pitched as experience, turned into a dynamic rather than passive activity. Attempting to represent a work (dancing *Trio A*) with our own bodies, alongside that work's historical document (the video recording of Yvonne Rainer dancing *Trio A*) is interesting and relates to themes of failure, or to the attempt, which run throughout the piece.

Hanging a work from the Tate collection, on the other hand, became like an enquiry into the institution. It became a way of making manifest our engagement with the museum, of positioning ourselves within it and trying to understand the implications of that – 'finding our weight' as Pat Catterson, our dance teacher, would have said.

Are there stories behind the objects you are showing in the exhibition space?

The reason for making the programme notes available, and for the titles of the individual works in the gallery, is to make it clear that these objects might come from biographical sources, but biographical narrative is not their content. On one level a kind of personal change has occurred for both of us, but this is private, in the same way as those people with whom we have negotiated the hanging of the work of art at Tate might have been affected by that process. Both are about the possibility and validity of personal change, without the work needing to make this public in an explicit way. The work, as we said before, is the result of the process but is not necessarily its equivalent.

Could you describe what is at stake politically in the way that your work makes human relations manifest?

We would question the defining line between (physical) actions and (political) activism – between personal change, social change and activism, even. We have no message, but we are engaged in and hoping to give form to a process of exchange. Is it like making an address without a message? Is the performance like spending some time with people as we have spent time with each other?

We don't know. We could say we know that there are only people in relation to other people, and what is at stake between one person and another person? Maybe everything.

6 *Things we couldn't do, but can do now* 2004, performance at Tate Britain
Courtesy the artists

Jimmy Robert & Ian White 39

Muse 2004, production still
Courtesy the artist

Jananne Al-Ani
The Visit

Since the mid-1990s Jananne Al-Ani has developed a body of video and photographic work that has revolved around narrative, history and storytelling, and has often looked at Western representations of the Middle East. She has regularly used her mother and her three sisters, as well as herself, as performers. Their relationship to each other is never explicit, but their striking resemblance to one another and compelling intimacy has become a consistent motif in her work.

In response to the clichéd, exoticised depictions of women in late nineteenth-century Orientalist photography and painting, Al-Ani's photographic work has employed the visual motif of the veil to confront Western preconceptions of Middle Eastern society. In one series, *Untitled* 1996, Al-Ani showed herself, her mother and sisters sitting in a row, veiled to varying degrees, ranging from fully exposed to fully covered. While the veil appears and disappears, the focus remains on the women's eyes, and the powerful, confrontational nature of their stare, highlighting the way in which both male and female gazes are implicated by the veil.

Al-Ani's videos have often explored narratives based on memories and family histories, creating complex, cryptic dialogues that are played out by the five women in scripted vignettes. In *A Loving Man* 1996–9, the women play a memory game in which they recount a story constructed from different phrases gathered from each woman's account of their relationship to an absent man, combining them to reveal a tangled portrait of a troubled separation.

Presented in Art Now, Al-Ani's *The Visit* 2004 is a video installation in two parts. Projected onto a large floating screen, *Muse* opens with a shimmering heat haze that disperses to reveal an isolated man restlessly pacing over an empty patch of barren, windy desert. Dressed in a smart suit, the man appears as a kind of apparition seemingly displaced in the wide, open landscape, which shows no other signs of human presence. His movements are captured in seven short sequences, filmed over the course of one day, the passage of time marked by the gradual setting of the sun and the lengthening of his shadow. The creeping darkness and the frustrating repetition of his directionless movements create a distinct air of melancholy.

Behind a partition wall *Echo* presents the 'talking heads' of four women on separate screens, each speaking in an emotional, impassioned manner. The individual dialogues are played simultaneously, layered over one another to create a muddled murmuring, which prevents the viewer from grasping one single thread. Occasional isolated phrases pierce through the chatter, offering clues to the unravelling of the situation, conveying an abstract impression of loss and disappointment resulting from a visit that they all refer to. The story never evolves into complete sense, and while the anecdotal fragments seem to link the women to the mysterious man in the desert, no concrete relationship ever comes to light.

The juxtaposition of *Muse* and *Echo* creates a dichotomy between male and female space. Viewed from afar, the man's inhabitation of the transitory landscape of the desert gives him an apparent sense of freedom, but his space is controlled by the fixed viewpoint of the camera. The arid patch of wilderness becomes a stage across which he repeatedly performs, and where he eventually appears trapped. In contrast, the female subjects are presented on a more domestic, intimate scale. Filmed up close, they speak frankly and directly to the camera in a relaxed, informal manner. The documentary-like quality comes across as natural next to the staged cinematic grandeur of *Muse*. While the women express the story from their perspective, the man is not given a voice.

The desert itself is frequently depicted by Westerners as a magical, exotic, empty space. In *Muse* Al-Ani counteracts this by portraying her subject not in the idealised, romantic sweeping sand dunes that are usually associated with Western ideas of the desert, but in a generic, stony, dusty terrain. The film was in fact shot in the Middle East – a landscape that has become familiar to Westerners as the backdrop to military action, often seen in aerial views in the reportage of the two Gulf wars. In her essay *Acting Out*[1] Al-Ani describes the absence of the body in these representations:

> Through the portrayal of the population, the culture and, crucially, the landscape of the Middle East, [the news reportage] revealed that the nineteenth-century Orientalist stereotype of the Arab and the desert remained firmly embedded in Western consciousness. The site of the war was shown to be a desert, a place with no history and no population – an empty space, a blank canvas.

Al-Ani's *Muse* can in some ways be seen as humanising the desert by inserting a figure into the landscape.

In earlier works Al-Ani's explorations of the symbolic use of the veil highlighted it as an interface between public and private space, contrasting the exposure to the real with the realm of the imaginary that opens up once something is hidden from view. There is also an aspect of veiling in the way that Al-Ani tantalises the viewers of her work with the truth. Fragments of reality linger in the background, such as the involvement of her family, and in the case of *The Visit*, her choice of a location that has complex associations.

Similarly, the warmth and candour of her sisters' performances make it difficult to believe that they are not acting out their own story. She subverts narratives by layering and dramatisation, which distance the truth and create a complex sense of ambiguity that blurs fact and fiction, never exposing the full picture. What her work does reveal is a powerful sense of the difficulties of family relationships, and the human consequences of war. Counteracting the often brash nature of media reportage, these lyrical works demonstrate how personal narratives and shared stories can accrue wider significance.

More recently, Al-Ani has been developing a new body of photographic and video work concerned with the 'disappearance' of the body from sites of violent contestation across the Middle East. The work brings together visuals collected

1. *Veil: Veiling, Representation and Contemporary Art*, exh. cat., inIVA in association with Modern Art Oxford, London, 2003, p. 90

from locations of conflict and atrocity across the region, historic material appropriated from photographic, film and sound archives, and a selection of first-person narratives relating to the selected sites. Together this material explores the internal workings of archives, the tension between collective and individual experience and the interrogation of the documentary tradition. By linking particular instances of war and genocide with personal conditions and subjective narratives, Al-Ani examines the notion of truth, challenges the authority of the narrator and highlights the fallibility of collective and individual memory. As the burgeoning debate on contemporary art practice from the Middle East continues to strengthen, Al-Ani investigates the artist's role as image-maker in confronting the conventions of reportage and the ever-increasing demand for explicit and abject images produced in zones of conflict.

Emily Pethick

The Visit 2004, installation views
Left: *Echo* 1994–2004; Right: *Muse* 2004

Courtesy the artist. Commissioned by Film and Video Umbrella and Norwich Gallery. Supported by Arts Council England, Film London, and the Henry Moore Foundation.

Tate New Hang 5 2004–5
Courtesy the artist and Maureen Paley, London

Tate New Hang 8 2004–5
Courtesy Tate. Purchased in 2006

Andrew Grassie
New Hang

Andrew Grassie is a painter whose starting point is a re-examination of the fundamental question of what to paint. He turns this question on its head, producing paintings which present a series of compelling propositions about painting itself, recording and representing scenarios such as the circumstances of their own production or display.

Grassie's Art Now exhibition, *New Hang*, consisted of thirteen small paintings. Each showed a different view of an exhibition in the space in which his paintings were exhibited, Tate Britain's Art Now room. This exhibition was made up of works from the Tate collection, including well-known paintings and sculptures by historic British artists such as George Stubbs and JMW Turner, international modern 'masters' such as Barnett Newman and Pablo Picasso, and works by two living artists, Bridget Riley and Bruce Nauman. Grassie's paintings were hung according to the view of the room that they depicted. Thus, a viewer looking at one of Grassie's pictures saw the space in which they were standing. They might also have noticed that the lighting in the room was exactly the same as in Grassie's paintings. This doubling – of the space in the paintings and the space which the viewer occupied – created an uncanny dislocation which questioned our sense of reality, space and illusion.

To make *New Hang* Grassie selected, at intervals, works from Tate's collection and installed them in the Art Now room between exhibitions. Having mapped out the space and established his viewpoints (and thus camera positions), Grassie photographed the same set of views each time a new group of works was installed. He then pieced together a set of images of the 'complete' exhibition: an impossible or, more accurately, implausible event. Then, working from these images, he painted the pictures that made up *New Hang*.

The title of the exhibition referred to the annual redisplay of the collection that used to take place at the Tate Gallery. The annual 'New Hang' was an opportunity to see familiar works in fresh curatorial contexts. Grassie's project offered a 'virtual' equivalent of such a re-display yet also challenged its methodology. Viewers might have questioned Grassie's choice of works, how they were displayed, and what readings and meanings emerged from the combinations he had pictured. In fact his choices were dictated simply by the desire to work with certain favourite artists and works and the formal demands of his compositions. He stressed that there was no curatorial intention in his selection or his 'hang'. Nonetheless, certain themes did emerge: contrasting depictions of the body in works by William Blake, Henry Moore, Hans Bellmer and Picasso, or the doubling seen in both Nauman's *Double No* and *The Cholmondeley Ladies*. Free from the burden of a curatorial agenda, Grassie enjoyed 'accidental' conjunctions such as the way Frederic Leighton's *Sluggard* seemed to be flaunting himself to Picasso's *Nude Woman in a Red Armchair*. He was also interested in the way works of art using such radically different languages of representation were brought together in his paintings, which in turn employed yet another form of pictorial language.

Grassie's way of working developed out of an impasse he found himself in while studying at the Royal College of Art. Under pressure to develop a 'signature' style, he worked his way through many stylistic models, eventually reaching what he felt was a dead end. His response to this was to start painting copies of his own work: a solution reminiscent of Samuel Beckett's resignation: 'I can't go on. I'll go on.' Yet Grassie found that in making what at first seemed like a kind of 'dumb' gesture – a wilfully negationist action in that it seemed to deny creativity – something new and interesting emerged. Grassie explained: 'My self-reflexive stance originated from the problem of what to paint, or rather how to justify it to myself. The technique of copying a photograph, rather than implying an interest in the 'photo-real', was simply a paring down to the bare bone of a practice. What emerged out of this discipline was surprisingly expansive and referential.' One might say that because of his doubt about the practice of painting, Grassie's work has developed as a way of providing him with excuses to make paintings.

Grassie's methods are relatively simple, if technically demanding, but from them emerges a complex and layered situation that can be misunderstood as a form of photorealism or appropriation. He has said: 'I am as much interested in the differences that occur in the "look" of my paintings from the photograph, and what this implies, as any proximity. They seem now to refer to the "silent gaze" of much seventeenth-century Dutch art and to certain forms of minimalism more than to photo-realism.' As this suggests, Grassie is engaged in a dialogue with art history. As well as methodologies of creation, exhibition and display, his work addresses a strand that runs throughout art history, of artists drawing on the work of their predecessors for inspiration. A parallel strand locates copying (initially as a means of instruction) as fertile ground. However, one should stress that work such as *New Hang* is not appropriation, for the works of art depicted are identified as real works within a real space and retain their original identity.

Grassie has furthered this enquiry more recently with projects exploring the contexts within which exhibitions are staged, including *Private* 2006 at Sperone Westwater, New York, and *Installation* 2006 at Maureen Paley, London. For *Private*, working once again from photographs, Grassie focused on behind-the-scenes spaces at the gallery, his small canvases showing glimpses

Private: Office 2006
Courtesy the artist and Sperone
Westwater, New York

Installation: Maaike Schoorel 2006
Courtesy the artist and
Maureen Paley, London

of works by fellow artists in offices, storage areas and hallways. For *Installation* Grassie documented the programme of exhibitions held at Maureen Paley's gallery in London in 2006, adhering to the mission statement: 'install a series of paintings at the gallery depicting the year's previous exhibitions during their installation. Each painting should hang at the very spot from which the image was taken, enabling the viewer to compare the views of the space.'

Grassie is a painter yet his practice suggests that we might consider his work in two further ways: as conceptual art, and as installation art. Sol Le Witt argued that the use of conceptual frameworks and self-imposed conditions 'eliminates the arbitrary, the capricious and the subjective as much as possible.' But Grassie has found that 'freedom from having to invent' actually means he can locate self-expression in other aspects of his work, in painterly qualities such as 'touch' for example. The thirteen paintings that comprised *New Hang* have been dispersed since the show closed. But in its complete form the exhibition existed as a single work which occupied (and activated) the space in which it was displayed. It was site-specific, made for the Art Now room. As such it was essentially an installation in which the component parts happened to be paintings.

Ben Tufnell

Tate New Hang 1 2004–5

Tate New Hang 7 2004–5

Tate New Hang 9 2004–5

Tate New Hang 13 2004–5

All images courtesy the artist and Maureen Paley, London

Andrew Grassie 51

John Peel 2004
Courtesy the artist and Cranford Collection, London

Michael Fullerton
Suck on Science

Michael Fullerton's practice explores the transmission and reception of information in its broadest sense, from the tools and technologies of communication to the institutions and individuals responsible for its generation and dispersal. Fullerton's line of enquiry translates into two apparently distinct bodies of work which appear to share little aesthetic common ground: paintings skilfully executed in the tradition of eighteenth-century English portraiture, and more obviously conceptual works that span sculpture, screen-prints and film. Presented as all-encompassing installations, collectively his work questions the role and responsibilities of the interpreter and the relationship between aesthetics and belief.

In *Suck on Science*, this relationship was articulated through the artist's ambiguous homage to chemical giants BASF, around whose manifesto of inventions the exhibition was framed. The company, famous for inventing magnetic tape in 1935 and industrialising the technology that established analogue recording in its modern form, in fact began life by pioneering the chemistry necessary for the mass production of pigments. Fullerton sees a neat parallel between the two innovations which in effect 'revolutionised' two different types of broadcasting technology.

For Fullerton, the painting process is analogous to a recording mechanism for which the artist claims ultimate responsibility. Once a subject has been selected, a host of aesthetic choices are necessary in shaping the image, in conveying intent. Aesthetic decisions therefore potentially represent political decisions with the power to produce an 'effect'. Fullerton's interest in the eighteenth-century painter Thomas Gainsborough stems from the role he played in documenting and reinforcing a social class that he would not have gained access to without the aesthetic component of his vocation, commenting: 'I like the idea of aesthetics symbolically underwriting the importance of politics.'

Fullerton's portraits often depict individuals who have become defined to some extent by their political convictions or commitment to a vision that followed through into action. *A Loyal Beautiful Aesthete For a World That Didn't Care* 2004 is a head-and-shoulders portrait of Michael Collins, who served a two-year prison sentence for his role in the anti-capitalist riots in London. Fullerton describes the work as a 'model' of painting, suggesting a link between the physical intervention taken by Collins and the force required to manipulate paint. *Ross McWhirter Aged 13 at the Outbreak of War* 2004 is a sepia rendition of the co-founder of the *Guinness Book of Records*, the world's bestselling book. McWhirter was an outspoken critic of the IRA, renowned for his right-wing beliefs, who was fatally shot in 1975. Fullerton's full-length portrait of John Peel, complete with jumper, cup of coffee and quizzical smile, exudes warmth and admiration for the late broadcaster and committed champion of the musical avant-garde.

Fullerton's paintings possess a ghostly, transient quality that is the very antithesis of the monumental portrait commission. Instead, his subjects emerge tentatively from the indistinct gloom of the background, through loose, soft brushwork that gradually gains definition around the features, humanising rather than elevating. This hesitancy may suggest Fullerton's desire to represent a quality beyond an accurate likeness and his persistent questioning of the painting process as his images slowly take shape. Underpinning all his investigations is an examination of whether aesthetic choices succeed in communicating values beyond the merely decorative.

This idea was further elaborated through sculptural works such as *Who Keeps the World Both Old and New, in Pain or Pleasure?* 2004. Comprising six four-metre-long poles suspended vertically from the ceiling on wires, the sculpture seems to reference a Minimalist vocabulary in its formal rigour. The work is, in fact, a scaled-up model of the rods of the human eye, the receptors of light, taken from an anatomy book, cast from mild steel and coated in one of BASF's latest pigments, 'magic purple' (the pigment shifts colour from orange to purple, depending on the angle from which it is viewed). Similarly its counterpart, two cones made of a mixture of urethane and ferric oxide (the raw material that stores signal on videotape), alludes to non-visible information contained beyond the visually pared-down surface of the objects. Fullerton's decision to position the cones either side of the original microphone used by the late Alistair Cooke to broadcast *Letter From America*, the world's longest-running speech radio programme, reinforced the notion of the objects as active mechanisms, of one thing influencing another.

Providing a backdrop to the installation was a grid of billboard sized silk-screened images on newsprint, based on a photograph of a room in the apartment of the controversial philosopher Nietzsche. In a sort of reversal of the painting process, Fullerton began with a complete image and, printing repeatedly until the ink ran out, subjected it to a level of distortion until it became unintelligible. For Fullerton, the progressive disintegration of the picture plane echoes the way in which Nietzsche's ideas have been variously appropriated and manipulated for political purposes beyond his original intention.

At the root of Fullerton's practice is an awareness of the mediated nature of the process of recording and the ways in which this information becomes open to distortion once out in the public arena. Thus, for Fullerton, the artist's role is a precarious one but at the same time one of the highest responsibility. Once out in the world and divorced from its context, the work is dependent on judgement from institutions and critics, often with other motivations, for its interpretation and validation. At the centre of the installation sat a large roll of blank newsprint. Titled *No Title ('silence is so ... accurate!' – Mark Rothko, 1947)* the work's mute objecthood offered an eloquent retort.

Lizzie Carey-Thomas

Suck on Science 2004, installation view

Michael Fullerton 55

*Ross McWhirter aged 13 at the outbreak of the War
(founder, Guinness Book of Records) 2004*

David Milligan 2004

fade held 2005, installation view

All works courtesy the artist and The Approach, London

Martin Westwood
fade held

Martin Westwood's sculptural installations and collages draw heavily on the slick world of big business for both subject matter and materials. Yet his aesthetic, which has developed from a background in painting, is curiously intricate and decorative; the use of bold colour and elaborate patterning are characteristic of his very particular approach to 'picture-making'. In both two and three dimensions, new environments are carefully composed by layering myriad images, forms and ideas that, through their juxtaposition and presentation, create tension by appearing both familiar and strange.

For several years, Westwood has developed a body of work that represents everyday scenes of retail, advertising and business, each populated by customers and company professionals engaged in moments of exchange or transaction. Figures like the car salesman and the suited executive are recognisable stereotypes of the commercial world. But Westwood depicts them with the anonymity of a generic performance. Flat, faceless and constructed from sterile materials, they are rendered unfamiliar, lifeless and dysfunctional.

Commerce and its effect on daily life is a constant theme in Westwood's work. The banality of corporate culture and the deadening effects of its streamlined and automated systems in a throwaway society are at the heart of his practice. Slick business brochures, industry magazines and commonplace mass-produced objects from the office and commercial environment provide him with the raw materials for his complex and multi-layered work. Old newspapers, photographs, invoice sheets, paperclips and pin boards are removed from their regular habitat and recycled, through an idiosyncratic process of destruction and reconstruction, to form highly crafted components of larger installations, such as Westwood's Art Now exhibition, *fade held* 2005. The impersonal nature of the media and Westwood's methods of production sets limits on his artistic role and perhaps redefines him as a participant in a larger network of processes rather than a sole, isolated creator.

Angelus Novus 2004, installation view, Collective Gallery, Edinburgh

Westwood's remodelling of the corporate aesthetic generates visually compelling elements that subtly undermine the order and uniformity of their origin. For example, the idealised form of the balloon – a festive object often commandeered as a promotional tool – is instantly recognisable throughout Westwood's work. But often, inverted and formed of a solid membrane, it becomes peculiar and attention is drawn to the process of its manufacture. Hand-made from shredded strips of paper meticulously pieced together as a papier-mâché sphere, Westwood's balloons put office waste to symbolic use. Shredded documents – sensitive or confidential data – are redeployed in new forms to charge the balloon with connotations of secrecy, weight and petrification. Viewed in the context of the installation *Angelus Novus* 2004, the ideas of artistic freedom and naivety associated with this childhood craft activity are tainted.

Westwood compounds the idea that creativity finds little outlet in a bureaucracy through his repeated use of natural forms, such as the leaf. In *fade held* 2005, machined from stainless steel and resembling a company logo, Westwood's thick, heavy leaves deny their organic origins. Having dropped to the ground they can be read as lugubrious and inert symbols of the fall of man in modern times. Similarly, in *Angelus Novus*, natural images, reworked as insignia on invoice sheets, were strewn across the floor like debris. In both they highlight the tension between spontaneity and control in commercial environments and make ironic comment on the corporate use of images from nature. The repetition of these elements throughout Westwood's work gives them the force of emblems. Collectively they establish a distinct iconography with which the artist skews normality and disrupts expectation.

Human figures and gestures are also pivotal to Westwood's work, and often underline the uneasy relationship between personal freedom and systems of control that exist within capitalist societies. In *fade held*, for instance, the group of figures, laser-cut from stainless steel, resembled cut-outs from a shop window. On an adjacent wall a credit card transaction took place at a cash desk, and a car – symbol of success and prestige – was stencilled next to its prospective buyer. The sanitised and anonymous representation of Westwood's figures dehumanises them. In his work individuality is expendable, identity measurable only in terms

Sunset Clause 2004

Death Spiral Converted 2007

of ownership. The notes and scraps of paper tacked to objects or stuffed into the gaps and joints of figures hint at hidden details and inner thoughts and heighten the sense of repression, the stranglehold of corporate goals over personal agency. In works such as *Sunset Clause* 2004 this theme is illustrated to the extreme as human forms are literally pinned down by a network of colourful map pins. A feeling of emptiness and alienation dominates these scenes of commerce and disrupts the sense of order expected in such arenas.

Typically, with no discernible narrative to unite his collection of figures and forms, Westwood directs the viewer's attention back to the physical details of his installations. In *Angelus Novus* the scale of the gallery was altered by a dropped ceiling, which accentuated the sense of a child-like place and reinforced the idea of the nursery environment. Similarly, the raised floor of *fade held*, accessed via a ramp, compressed the space and provided the gallery with a sense of theatre. Two temporary curved screens extending around the perimeter of the room added to the impermanence of the spectacle. Moreover, their dynamic colour and the geometric precision of other structural features were reminiscent of the early twentieth-century industrial aesthetic of Constructivism and made reference to Moholy-Nagy's commercial designs for temporary exhibition and trade stands.

The great variety of parts from which Westwood's displays are made up often undermines the initial appearance of order and uniformity. *fade held* was an unpredictable, open-ended environment, which invited the viewer to explore many different paths, to make links between its constituent objects and ideas. Advancing through the installation, the viewer's path was impeded by several spiral stairwells cut into the floor, each more abstracted and dynamic than the last. These structures, perhaps suggestive of flaws in a system, were at odds with architectural practice and the civilising idea of co-ordinated space. Resembling pie charts or Venn diagrams, they served to remind the viewer that the installation was constructed within an economic framework. Within the context of a national museum, such structures prompted consideration of actual physical surroundings and, suggesting parallels between cultural and commercial arenas, questioned what might be beneath the surface of this temporary structure, or indeed behind the façade of the institution.

fade held 2005, installation view

Westwood continues to explore the effects of a businesslike approach to art in more recent work such as *Death Spiral Converted* 2007: a circular display table containing hundreds of small paper discs revealing photocopied faces, piled up at the sides of the case like shingle washed up on a beach. These most recent exhibits appear less hand-crafted and more refined in finish, almost as if Westwood's own methods of production are mimicking the systems he critiques. A similar display table, *Hold* 2005, formed the centrepiece of *fade held*. Encased behind glass, outmoded images of a man and a woman were held down by stone-like lumps fabricated from low-grade materials. The objects were given a new status and value by virtue of their being on display, and yet were at the same time deadened. The Venn diagram shape was repeated in *Hold* and solidified to provide the tabletop. While reminiscent of an eclipse, the two-tone glass from which the top was made revoked any romance associated with such natural phenomena. A transitional moment was held in check. Cast into darkness, the interaction between the figures below the glass surface and the suggestion of intimacy remained hidden and contained.

Throughout Westwood's work, the presence of an unpredictable force is discernable: the stone that weighs down a sheet of paper on a table, strands of hair blown across a customer's face, the scattering of fallen leaves across a space. All these details suggest freedom and evoke the disordering power of the wind, throwing all things human or man-made into sharp contrast. Ultimately, all of Westwood's investigations remain open-ended. With normality disrupted, his installations function as psychological spaces, a stage on which a chain of fundamental contradictions of contemporary life are played out to allow a moment for reflection.

Rachel Tant

50ft queenie 2005, installation views
All works courtesy greengrassi, London, and Galerie Daniel Buchholz, Cologne

Silke Otto-Knapp
soft queenie

For her exhibition at the 2005 Istanbul Biennial Silke Otto-Knapp installed
a group of paintings depicting female figures in the faded art-deco grandeur
of the almost-derelict Deniz Palas apartments, which overlook the Golden Horn.
Presented unframed on cracked and flaking walls, in rooms with bare floorboards,
drenched in daylight from the windows, Otto-Knapp's paintings seemed at once
to belong both to a vanished era – the luxurious world which the apartments would
have epitomised in their early twentieth-century heyday – and the quotidian,
immediate present. The apartments seemed to offer perfect viewing conditions for
the paintings, enhancing both their symbolic complexity and their fleeting surface
beauty. For Otto-Knapp's recent paintings have an unsettling – and beguiling –
tendency to disappear before our eyes. As we move before them and our point
of view changes the light catches brushstrokes, pigments and metallic surfaces.
The images alternately come into existence and dissolve into their surroundings,
an effect that photographic reproduction cannot possibly capture. They seem
to embody a complex matrix of past and present, artificiality and reality, memory
and history. They are also, for the artist, personal explorations of her imagery and
the image-making process. They enact a balancing act in which the overt subject
(the dancers) and the implicit subject (the question of painting and what it might
mean) co-exist.

German-born Otto-Knapp has been based in London since 1995. Working
with watercolour, she has developed an international reputation for her paintings
of landscapes and figures. Her recent work represents a departure. While her
subjects suggest a continuation of earlier themes, she has transformed the
appearance of her work by producing almost-monochrome paintings in silver
and gold, colours associated with sophistication and spectacle, but also illusion
and artificiality.

Otto-Knapp's past subjects have included the botanic gardens and glasshouses
at Kew, Los Angeles cityscapes, Las Vegas hotels, Busby Berkeley musicals,
and performers such as PJ Harvey and Patti Smith, subjects in which a tension
between artifice and reality is both manifest and blurred. This tension is a key
theme of Otto-Knapp's work. While it might seem that she is drawn to highly
romantic subjects she is in fact interested in (partially) defusing this romantic
aura. Her work thus negotiates a series of contradictions. It is at once intense
and 'cool', simultaneously traditional and concerned with the process of its own
production, both formal and mysterious.

Otto-Knapp's recent paintings are derived from found photographs documenting
dance performances. A number are inspired by images of Igor Stravinsky's *Les
Noces*, which was written for Diaghilev's *Ballet Russes* and first performed in Paris
in 1923 with costumes by the Russian painter Natalia Goncharova. *Les Noces*
was choreographed by Bronislava Nijinska and it was the compositions that
she developed, coupled with Goncharova's simple and striking costumes,
that attracted Otto-Knapp. Nijinska's choreography was described as 'austere'

and 'monumental' and the movements of the dancers – stilled in the photographs that Otto-Knapp works from – create powerful archetypal statements. However, although these paintings may take dance as their subject, they are not *about* dance. The formal, abstract, ritual aspects of ballet are translated in the painting process into formal, abstract pictorial statements; they provide a framework within which the artist can develop a dialogue with her materials. Thus her titles usually offer generic descriptions of the imagery, rather than identifying specific sources or hinting at a narrative. Nonetheless, these images, in which figures reach out for each other, lean together, or enact stylised gestures and expressions, do retain the ability to convey a sense of human drama. It is this tension that makes them so compelling.

For this series of paintings Otto-Knapp has worked from production photographs (often themselves mediated by photocopying or over-painting). However, in these works one sees a curious reversal taking place: the images retreat beyond the source photographs and approach the condition of the costume designs that preceded them. In part this is due to the reduced technique Otto-Knapp has used. In contrast to her highly textured earlier work, in which paint is drawn, brushed, poured, dripped, splashed and washed, many of these recent paintings display a hard, flat, graphic style. Her use of silver and gold paint enhances this, creating an impersonal, metallic surface.

Watercolour is a medium that, in Britain especially, has a venerable history and contested status. While Otto-Knapp is familiar with British artists such as Turner, Girtin, Blake and Rossetti her decision to work in watercolour was prompted not by a desire to engage with the history and traditions of the medium, but by a process of formal experimentation. Working on prepared canvas instead of paper allows her to use the paint in a new way: rather than soaking into the ground it pools on and drips down the surface. Otto-Knapp has explained:

> Painting on canvas enables me to rework the picture in order to connect the drawn and painted elements, and to develop a complex space. The transparency and ephemeral nature of the watercolours makes the picture appear as if it is floating on the surface of the canvas. As the paint dries, shapes and edges develop which I can't necessarily predict beforehand, but which I then react to. Watercolours dry quickly so I almost have to act on the offensive in working with this residue and the 'coincidences'.

The finished painting is thus as much about the process of arriving at a resolution of pictorial incident as it is about articulating an idea about a person, place or event. However, process does also create meaning. In repeatedly washing down her images, reworking them layer by layer, Otto-Knapp is able to create pictures of great translucency, delicacy and beauty. But they can also imply violence, obliteration or decay. In some works it is as if the artist has attempted to erase the subject, leaving just a trace. Thus the *Queen of the night (after Bakst)* and other figures seem to be on the verge of disappearing, as if fading back into history.

Ben Tufnell

soft queenie 2005

Portrait 2005

Two figures facing 2005

The bride's chamber scene 2005

Above: *In Search of Perfect Harmony* 2006, installation view
Below: *In Search of Perfect Harmony* 2003–6 (detail)
All works courtesy the artist and Haunch of Venison, London

Jamie Shovlin
In Search of Perfect Harmony

Jamie Shovlin is a collector, an obsessive accumulator of material and information. He makes work about anything that interests him: however, the perception of information remains a constant premise for his practice. His carefully structured projects are the result of in-depth research, idiosyncratic methodologies and painstaking execution, presenting layers of information and imagery that situate objects, people and ideas into new contexts. By using conventional models of presentation – the museum collection, archive, literary compendia – Shovlin questions how information manifests itself as authoritative. He explores the way that individuals and organisations map, classify and pigeon-hole the world in order to understand it.

Shovlin's Art Now exhibition, *In Search of Perfect Harmony* 2006, developed out of a larger proposal for his touring show *Aggregate* 2003–7. It began with, amongst other things, a fascination for an unlikely figure, the eighteenth-century curate Gilbert White. White led an unassuming life in the village of Selbourne, Hampshire, meticulously recording his observations of the wildlife in his garden and local surroundings. Despite his somewhat parochial view of nature, White is often remembered among the great pioneers of science and regarded as England's first ecologist. His writings were published in 1789 as *The Natural History and Antiquities of Selbourne*, now purportedly the fourth most published book in the English language. It is trivia such as this that sparks Shovlin's imagination. The accuracy of the anecdote is perhaps of less consequence than the intrigue it sustains. Inconsequential fact-finding feeds his creative thinking over a period of months and years, enabling him to form a complex web of associations that motivate his intricately constructed projects.

The installation, *In Search of Perfect Harmony* 2006, took nature as its theme and brought together drawings, collage, text, sound recording and projection. With its dark green walls, mahogany-framed exhibits and archival boxes, the display recalled the *Wunderkammer*, or a cabinet of curiosities one might encounter in a local museum. Shovlin juxtaposed his mother's subjective view of the wildlife in her suburban garden with the scientific rigour of Charles Darwin's theory of natural selection. Interested by how museums are organised and often evolve from diverse, personal collections, Shovlin's exhibition opposed an individual voice with an institutional point of view, contrasting localised knowledge with something much more global. Like Gilbert White, he reminded the viewer that the origins of science were based on very personal observation and endeavour.

Presentation is paramount for Shovlin. He works across different media adopting a hybrid role of researcher, artist, curator and archivist to free up huge creative potential. Authorial distance is exploited to investigate multiple points of view within a single project. Yet his art is characterised by a superficial 'authenticity', a look and feel that persuades the viewer to interpret his documents, charts and drawings as hard fact or historical evidence. *Naomi V. Jelish* 2001–4, for example, comprises an archive of drawings, scrapbooks, photographs and cuttings that purportedly document the life and work of a 13-year-old artist-prodigy from Kent who mysteriously disappeared without trace in July 1991 along with her entire family. One might expect to encounter a far-fetched story such as this sensationalised in a tabloid newspaper or gossip magazine, where it would be easy to overlook and dismiss. But Shovlin sustains interest in this improbable narrative through the format of its presentation. Although the hoax is not difficult to detect – the girl's name being an anagram of 'Jamie Shovlin' – the mode of display encourages the suspension of disbelief, illustrating one's general disinclination to question information that appears 'authoritative'.

Shovlin has continued to explore elaborate fictional constructions in more recent work such as *Lustfaust: A Folk Anthology 1976–1981* 2003–6. Here fanzines, bootleg album covers and rock memorabilia serve to commemorate an experimental noise band active in Berlin in the late 1970s and early 1980s. With this work, Shovlin distances himself from the conceit by adopting a visible curatorial stance. Moreover, complemented by 'live' elements such as video interviews and the Lustfaust website, this fiction is perhaps considered more plausible. But as Francesco Manacorda has described: 'Shovlin is not so much interested in convincing the viewer of the verity of the universe he is forging, but rather aims at seducing us to step into a fictional alternate world, and momentarily suspend our disbelief as we do at the cinema or when reading literature.'[1]

This idea of personal obsessions forming the basis of a fictional world in which the viewer can participate was central to Shovlin's Art Now installation. *The Twitcher* 2004–6 represented material about his mother Valerie and her musings on the inhabitants of the garden she had created and nurtured. A slide show of the garden progressed through the seasons while amateur footage of a 'traumatic' sparrow-hawk attack was projected onto a paving slab. The garden was mapped by a museological chart and taxonomic drawings documenting the occupants' scientific and more subjective habits. A fragmented soundtrack played in the space and affectionate, anthropomorphised accounts of 'Roger the Wood-Pigeon' and 'Dave the Collard Dove' were pieced together from a splintered monologue. Shovlin described his mother's relationship with her garden as 'maternal' and, as sound and image were reconnected by the viewer, the twicher's classification system was gradually revealed.

For Shovlin, the garden is analogous to a stage-set of characters; tensions between fantasy and reality are played out when predators upset the reassuring structure imposed on this corner of the natural world. On an allegorical level such futile attempts to tame nature link back to Darwin's theory of the 'survival of the fittest' as explored in *The Origin of Species* 1859 and reiterated in Shovlin's text piece of the same title. Here an apparently comprehensive view of chapter III, 'Struggle for Existence', was wall-mounted using pages from multiple, second-hand editions exchanged by Shovlin with universities and anonymous 'public' readers. However, each page was edited by Shovlin and any text not highlighted as important by previous readers was obliterated with thick black lines of ink.

1. Francesco Manacorda, 'Jamie Shovlin', *Beck's Futures 2006*, exh. cat., Institute of Contemporary Arts, London, 2006.

Naomi V. Jelish 2001–4,
installation view,
Riflemaker, London

The process Shovlin applied to the material echoes Darwin's theories and by
equating the survival of the fittest with the preservation of noteworthy text,
he questions the nature of 'valuable' or 'significant' information. Indeed, Darwin's
publication was subject to continuous revisions during and after his life and
as Shovlin comments: 'the different editions of the books, the edited versions
of history reported within the books, the history of the books as both source
of information and object, all collide in an effort to delineate – or highlight –
the impossible task of establishing the definitive history'.

Shovlin reinforced the idea of subjectivity and selectivity in his piece *In Search
of Perfect Harmony* 2003–6. This work comprised archival boxes displaying
frottages (wax rubbings using four overlaid colours) taken from jigsaws that
Shovlin's mother completed, almost subconsciously, whilst bird-watching.
Shovlin has noted that the majority of Valerie's jigsaws are utopian in subject and
illustrate idealised natural themes. But as the jigsaws are immediately collapsed
when finished, it would seem that the image is less important to her than the act
of completion itself. Shovlin's frottages provided a record of the jigsaw's structure
and pattern of construction without representing its image, leaving their titles
as the only means of accessing each 'harmonious' natural scene by means of
imagination. With reference to his own creative and somewhat absurdist methods
Shovlin alluded to the irony and futility of such ideal pursuits. A flawed system,
his Crayola colour wheel and an esoteric use of four-colour 'tetrads' were
employed to test the theory that complementary colours complete each other
when overlaid, producing a perfect neutral grey. Indeed, the production of only
30 frottages (that were anything but grey) from a possible 720 colour
combinations indicated the limitations of objective investigation.

As is typical with Shovlin's work, *In Search of Perfect Harmony* saw pseudo-
scientific structures subverted by fantasy. Bird-watching, Darwinism, jigsaw
puzzles and colour theory were merged by Shovlin but a resolution remained
unattainable. Functioning at the discretion of the viewer, the installation suggested
that ultimately 'perfect harmony' is illusory.

Rachel Tant

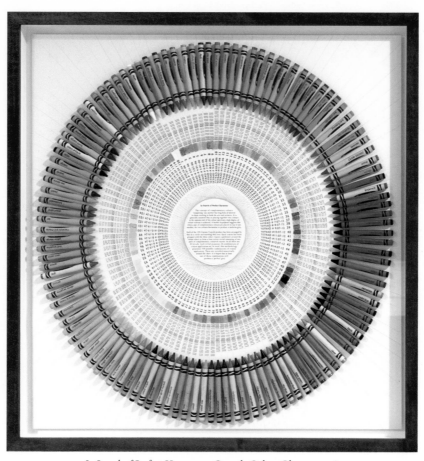

In Search of Perfect Harmony – Crayola Colour Chart 2003–6

ROGER
Wood-Pigeon
Columba palumbus

The Twitcher Plate 8 – Roger the Wood-Pigeon 2003–6

Stills from *Parres I* 2004
Courtesy the artist, Galeria OMR, Mexico City and Galerie Peter Kilchmann, Zurich

Melanie Smith
Parres – Trilogy

British artist Melanie Smith has lived in Mexico City since 1989. Her first-hand experience of the contradictions inherent in the world's third largest megalopolis undergoing rapid economic and cultural expansion – poverty and commerce, chaos and functionality, grime and beauty – is intrinsic to her practice. Fascinated by the ways in which historic and commercial influences translate into colour, materials and objects evident in the city's streets, Smith takes a formalist approach to revealing the underlying structures, visual excesses and social behaviours of this specific urban context. Her work takes a wide variety of forms, encompassing installation, photography and video, but is fundamentally informed by her background in painting and, more specifically, her ambivalence towards the legacy of twentieth-century abstraction.

Smith's view fluctuates from macro to micro, from the air to the ground. In *Spiral City* 2002, a camera attached to a helicopter swoops over the ever-spreading, regulated grid of streets while her series of photographs, *Tianguis* 1998–2002, draws attention to the brightly coloured impromptu tarpaulin structures erected by street vendors, which punctuate the grey surroundings like minimalist sculptural forms. For the series *Orange Lush* 1994 Smith tracked the most synthetic, abundant and seductive of colours throughout the city, gathering mass-produced plastic objects and presenting them as monochrome assemblages. For Smith, the colour orange is synonymous with authority, artifice and the industrialisation of the city. Smith has commented that she wants people to use 'abstraction as a point of departure from the reality of what they are actually seeing'.

Since 1997, Smith has collaborated with Rafael Ortega on a number of film and video projects that shift attention away from the finished artwork to the processes behind its production. These works seem to negate abstraction's drive towards

Orange Lush 1994
Courtesy the artist, Galeria OMR
and Mexico City

Stills from *Parres II* 2004
Courtesy the artist, Galeria OMR, Mexico City and Galerie Peter Kilchmann, Zurich

Spiral City 2002
Courtesy the artist, Galeria OMR,
Mexico City

a timeless autonomy by rooting it in a specific corporeal present. For example,
Six Steps towards Reality 2002 draws attention to the absurd quantities of energy
and labour required to achieve the appearance of effortless aesthetic 'purity'.
Six large, white projected images alluding to a reductive minimalist environment
shot from small polystyrene models on 16mm film are juxtaposed with handheld
video footage showing excerpts of the making of these images in Smith's studio.
The aloof, seamless image, divorced from context, seems far removed from the
circumstances of its making; the camera crew, equipment and sounds of banging,
chatter and laughter. Similarly, *Six Steps to a Project* 2004, shot in a cantina in
Mexico City, documents the making of a one-minute action involving film extras
that never actually gets made. Smith and Ortega's new trilogy of films *Parres I*
2004, *Parres II* 2004 and *Parres III* 2005, shown together for the first time in
Art Now, further explores the construction and breakdown of pictorial illusion.
Each is set in the small town of Parres, located just beyond the ever-encroaching
outskirts of Mexico City, and shot on 35mm film, instilling the imagery with
a cinematic depth. Smith and Ortega use the most basic units of filmmaking,
one camera and one roll of film, allowing the action to unfold in real time but
underscoring the artifice of the process by preserving the tail ends of footage.
The audio plays an important role in both sustaining and questioning the illusion
and has been recorded and edited specifically for each film.

In *Parres I* 2004, a man walks towards the camera along a road winding out
of a messy urban conurbation. As he approaches the camera he picks up a spray
paint gun and begins to coat the screen with a fine white mist, moving rhythmically
from left to right. As the layers of paint accumulate, the view beyond gradually
obscures until the shadow of the protagonist's arm against the opaque surface
replaces his own image. Smith notes how the action creates a shift away from any
narrative connotations implied by the setting into the realms of performance and
then pictorial abstraction. A sombre melody sung by a lone female accompanies
the imagery, as if mourning for the forgotten landscape beyond.

Parres II 2004 follows a similar scenario. The opening frames focus on
a close-up of a woman's blinking eye. The camera slowly retreats backwards

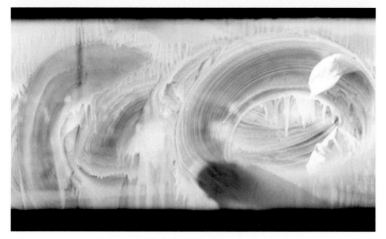

Stills from *Parres III* 2004
Courtesy the artist, Galeria OMR, Mexico City, and Galerie Peter Kilchmann, Zurich

to locate the figure in a waterlogged urban scrubland. She clutches a blue and pink woven plastic shopping bag, colours echoed in her pink top and the blue-painted building behind. In tandem with the camera's movement a heavy downpour rapidly bleaches out the scene until all that remains is a milky, streaky blur. As with *Parres I* 2004, a melancholy song accompanies the imagery, which stops abruptly as the rain clears and clarity is restored.

Parres III 2005 offers an exact reversal of the previous two films. A painted grey plane fills the screen which is slowly broken down by the actions of a window cleaner. There is a discernible pleasure to be had in tracing the drips of water and gestural smears of his cloth as the picture surface gradually deteriorates. As both the landscape beyond and the protagonist become visible through the glass the amplified sloshing sound of cloth being dipped in water is replaced by ambient village noises of dogs barking and a brass band playing mournfully in the distance. The unmistakable whirring sound of the camera takes over as the protagonist turns his back to the screen and walks towards the village, reinforcing the fact that we are observing a fiction.

In each of the *Parres* films the visible world is hidden by or revealed behind a monochrome image. Smith describes monochrome painting as, 'the exemplification of a kind of detached open window through which the spectator's gaze passes in search of transformation.' Collectively, the trilogy seems to succinctly articulate the ambiguities present within Smith's work; the complex dichotomy between the pursuit of the aestheticised image against the backdrop of contemporary urban life.

Lizzie Carey-Thomas

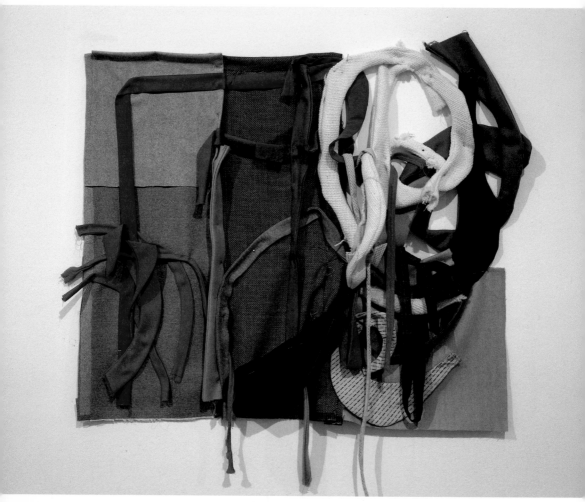

Wall Hanging #1 2006

All works courtesy the artist and greengrassi, London

Karin Ruggaber
From hard to soft

As part of a group of wall-based pieces made and brought together for the Art Now exhibition, Ruggaber produced tile-like shapes using experimental and often deliberately unpredictable casting processes that mixed dissonant elements such as cement, plaster and fabric. These densely worked layers of materials, textures and colour tones were configured into small groups, emphasising the tactile quality of the individual elements. Made primarily from man-made materials, these constructed relief pieces allude to cartoonish and geometric shapes but stay just outside of representational forms. In other works artificial and natural fabrics were pinned or sewn together to create a complex collage of shapes and forms, reminiscent of tailored elements associated with details of clothing. By placing these varied works in close proximity to each other on one side of the gallery and using the wall's full height, the act of display was emphasised and became a focus for the exhibition.

Architecture, or more generally the organised urban environment, has been a consistent source of reference for Ruggaber, in particular the tactile quality of surfaces and the exterior fronts of buildings. She states, 'The relief pieces come from an interest in façades, erosion, and incongruity of surface. They contain a sense of this physicality. The façade as actual and as representational skin, in that its materiality speaks about the status of a building or content of it, as well as structurally holds together and differentiates between inside and outside.' The concrete surfaces of the reliefs are corrupted and destabilised by the apparently casual introduction of a swatch of tweed or a cutting of acid-coloured nylon. These additions of colour and texture acknowledge the vocabulary of the ornamental – albeit a rough and unfinished sense of the decorative. The process of making the pieces is a deliberate relinquishing of control; they are built up through juxtaposing something hard against something soft, something heavy against something weightless, light against dark, bright against sombre.

In selecting her fabric, Ruggaber looks for what she describes as different 'dynamics' or 'speeds' of fabric – heavy, traditional, warm tweeds or lodens against acidic-coloured nylons and acrylics, or airtex fabrics designed to be breathable, sporty, lightweight – colours and fabrics that have a functional purpose outside of fashion. Previous works took on the form of bags but sat on the borderlines of functionality, made up of elaborate and entangled straps and handles that deployed the vocabulary of bags but denied actual use. Ruggaber is intrigued by the techniques and language of tailoring: the detailing on a man's shirt, a collar shape, or how it sits upon a shoulder, describing a body or posture – 'the way certain fabrics fall, sit, move.' She is interested in 'fabric as a physical structure and what it represents through subtle detail … each fabric describes and carries with it a tradition through material, colour, shade, sheen, tone.' Just as the concrete reliefs denote the physicality of architectural surfaces that in turn are indicative of a building's

Overleaf: *From hard to soft* 2006

content or status, so her fabric pieces abstractly allude to the body and its activities through the material itself rather than in form. They are reminiscent of the strange density of tapestry or medieval coats of arms where disparate elements are pushed up against each other, competing in a confined space. These fragments of sewn or pinned cloth are assembled and organised on the same plane, at once two and three-dimensional.

The title of the Art Now show, *From hard to soft*, suggested, perhaps playfully, a sense of order or system for the act of displaying these objects indicating a spectrum of different consistencies, states or viewpoints. Ruggaber often selects titles that have: 'a contrast and energy within them or are slightly provocative or almost kitsch … [They] offer an angle at the work, they take on a role within the show, almost like a material, acting like a framing element, often simply introducing another element or image within it.' Ruggaber also makes artists' publications, and a new edition, bearing the same name, was published at the same time as the exhibition. The images used in these books, such as in the recent *Istanbul buildings and materials* 2005, explore similar preoccupations to the sculptural pieces – of colour, texture or how light hits a surface – so that each body of work parallels and informs the other. As with the objects the material presence of the books is of paramount importance; often different weights, types of printing and textures of paper are employed.

These images, which at times have become part of an exhibition, are taken primarily to record and document details, places or a feel of a situation. They can either be solarised or too dark, or awkwardly off-centre, deliberately disregarding aesthetic decisions or even basic rules of photography. 'I like taking images against the sun: some images are dark, under- or overexposed, reflections – this disturbs or interrupts the image in some way, distances it.' The pictures often contain different layers, patterns, contrasts of light and shade, blocks of colour, reflections and contrasting viewpoints. They reveal a particularly visual and visceral language that transcends across all of Ruggaber's works and that is ultimately resistant to verbal translation.

Katharine Stout

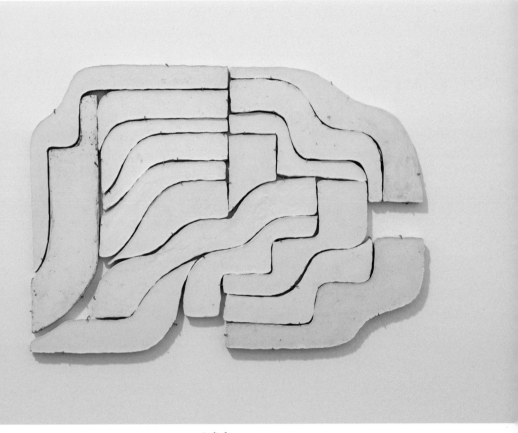

Relief #20 2006

Installation view
Courtesy the artist and Deitch Projects, New York

Raqib Shaw

Against the rich blue of a deep underwater world, strange mythical sea creatures –
half human, half animal – copulate and struggle together amongst glittering coral
reefs and shimmering shoals of fish; small ferocious sea creatures chase winged
penises ejaculating lines of silver; a black silhouetted human figure throws back
his bird head in painful ecstasy as he is straddled by an oversize lobster. *Garden
of Earthly Delights X* 2004 is the extraordinary centrepiece of a series of work by
Raqib Shaw which, unlike Hieronymous Bosch's fifteenth-century triptych of the
same title, seems to celebrate pleasure and the indulgence of sexual fantasy without
any recourse to moral codes or to a sense of reality. This labour-intensive painting
captivates and overwhelms the eye with its vivid hues, intricate detail and jewel-like
surface that initially mask the strong violence and sexuality of the imagery. Gold
stained-glass paint is used to outline each fictional character or detail and metallic
industrial paints fill in the intense colour range. Shaw's non-traditional techniques
and hybrid style are hard to place within contemporary art and culture, and yet
the work feels uniquely fresh and urgent.

Some writing on Shaw's work neatly positions it in terms of his Kashmiri
upbringing as part of 'a family of carpet makers'. Yet this is to reduce the work
to a neo-colonial notion of 'Otherness', echoing Shaw's impression of being treated
upon arrival at a London art school in 1998 as a 'noble savage'. As he points out:
'My work has nothing to do with what Kashmir stands for because as a child I had
so many influences. My parents are Muslim, my teachers were Hindu scholars,
I went to a Christian school and historically Kashmir was Buddhist. And then I was
living in India and it's very secular… and I didn't believe in organised religion. But
there is a great tendency in the West to say that you come from here so you must be
doing this and that.' The work is not representative of or affiliated to any particular
religious, geographical or ethnic influence, just as the artist's life story is more
complex and eventful than the summary often provided. Instead, Shaw's work is
a joyful conglomeration of styles and cultures colliding within a hedonistic mix.

However, although a biographical reading may be too literal, the subject of
each painting or work on paper can be seen as indicative of Shaw's emotional state
of mind at the time of production. The *Reflections* series of works on paper is
painted in his signature painstaking method of outlining each motif in gold, then
filling in the opulent colour; one mistake in the lengthy process and the whole thing
has to be abandoned. The series depicts a collection of witty and provocative coded
portraits of significant people in Shaw's life and betrays its preoccupation in the
title, offering an opportunity for the artist to contemplate the next direction for
his work. This partly took the form of translating a recurring two-dimensional
vignette, the repellent yet intriguing lobster/birdman found in *Garden of Earthly
Delights X*, into a sculpture. The exquisitely carved humanoid figure, a mirror
representation of Shaw's own physique, is made repulsive by the addition of
a stuffed turkey head. The predatory lobster, meticulously remodelled from an
actual creature to look convincingly realistic, is embellished with precious stones
embedded in the shell to make a surface at once beautiful and grotesque.

Like Shaw's paintings, this work uses the veneer, or even the actual materials, of wealth and extravagance to question the values of an expensive lifestyle, as it remains unclear whether the figures are conjoined in sexual celebration or abuse.

Responding to the Holbein exhibition at Tate Britain that coincided with his Art Now show, Shaw presented new works on paper and a painting that were inspired by this influential English Renaissance artist. *The Ambassadors* at the National Gallery was the first Western painting Shaw saw upon his arrival in London at the age of sixteen. He describes how his encounter with this celebrated portrait consolidated his growing reservations about entering the family business: 'I was very moved to see Holbein's *Ambassadors* as the painting seemed to answer my doubts about the meaning of life dedicated to making money.' Shaw is drawn to the morality tales of medieval and Renaissance art, just as he is excited by their antiquated techniques and artistic conventions in his drive to question what painting can be today. Though well informed about modernist art movements, their particular preoccupations – often more highly regarded in Western art history than elsewhere – are not especially relevant to him. It is significant that Holbein was an acclaimed designer of goldsmiths' work, jewellery and tapestry, amongst other skills, in an age when there was little distinction between the decorative and fine arts. With equal attention to the fine detail that conveys affluence and status, Shaw has reverently copied Holbein's iconic portraits of Henry VIII and wives Jane Seymour and Anne of Cleves and playfully embellished them with dramatic explosions and animal features. What may seem to some like a desecration is regarded by Shaw as homage as he appropriates Holbein to make work that reveals a period of personal turmoil in its unexpected violence. By adding his own theatrical features to these images he emphasises how they have now come to symbolise these historic figures, suggesting: 'I am very interested in the inevitable decrepitude of body and mind that is the human condition and the portraits, like everything else, are mere pegs to hang other issues on. I am also aware that Henry and Holbein have been dead for centuries and so will we pass away, but the symbols remain.'

The 'other-worlds' presented in Shaw's imaginative works are almost completely informed by an extensive knowledge and fascination with culture, whether popular, classical, ancient or modern, rather than an attempt to represent everyday life or a notion of reality. The artist comments: 'Since childhood there is a persistent confusion or even collision between stereotypes of reality and fantasy (whatever reality means) in my mind.' The eclectic sources that influence Shaw range from Hindu religious iconography to early Renaissance painters; from eighteenth-century travellers' journals in the archives of the Natural History Museum to a particular genre of British adult comics. Shaw appears to 'collect' cultural styles in much the same way as the Victorians did – as demonstrated in his extensive private collection of nineteenth-century porcelain – as a way to understand the world and his place within it. Beneath the mesmerising surfaces of Shaw's work, carefully calculated to seduce, lies a more subversive set of interests that seek to question the very ideals of decadence and luxury that they at first appear to represent.

Katharine Stout

Maquette 2006 (foreground); *Altarpiece* 2006 (background)
Courtesy the artist and Deitch Projects, New York

Left to right: *Jane* 2006; *Henry VIII* 2006; *Anne* 2006
Courtesy the artist and Deitch Projects, New York

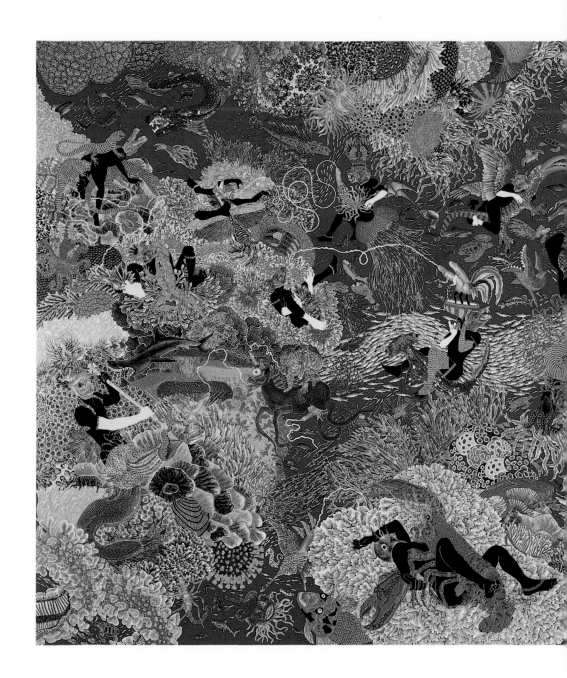

Garden of Earthly Delights X 2005
Collection of The Museum of Modern Art, New York. Gift of Adam Sender and George Lindemann Jr., 2005

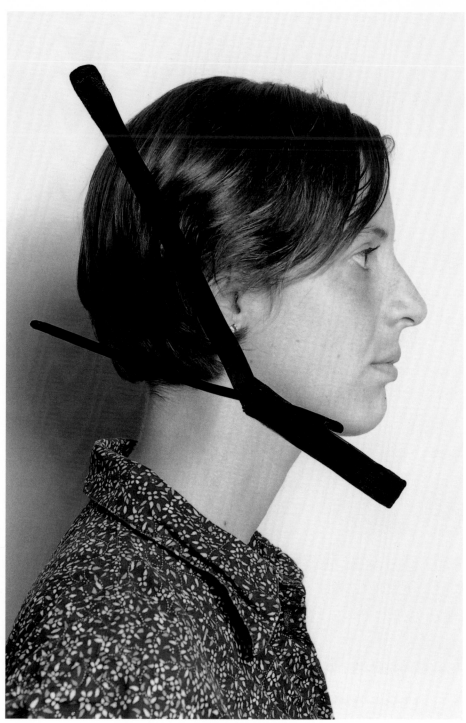

Your body is a battleground still (photo series 1–13) 2007, (detail)
All works courtesy the artist and Sorcha Dallas, Glasgow

Kate Davis
Your body is a battleground still

Kate Davis's carefully structured environments incorporate drawings, collages and sculptural objects. Linking each component is a connection to the body: whether subject to fragmentation and distortion through delicate pencil drawings, literally depicted in photographs, or obliquely suggested through a range of adapted and anthropomorphised readymade objects. These objects often resonate with domestic associations – a door handle, ladder or vase, for example – or relate to the technological enhancement of human potential – a bicycle or microphone. Taken out of context, modified or remade with unlikely materials, they appear at once defamiliarised and loaded with sensory connotations. Furthermore, the human and inanimate are often placed in direct material juxtaposition – flesh against wood or ceramic – or, in common with Surrealist motifs, fused to form hybrid beings, half-man, half-machine.

Davis's recent works have increasingly made reference to specific twentieth-century artists in both style and subject. Her 2006 exhibition *I want to function in the present time* produced an unlikely marriage between Kathe Kollwitz and Carl Andre, paying homage to their original ideas while reclaiming their vocabulary as something entirely her own. Davis comments: 'I suppose [my] process begins with a relatively open search and then hones in on a very specific kind of mark-making and the associations that those marks have acquired through art history. The question for me is how I can use my interpretation of those marks to say something today.'[1]

Davis's project for Art Now offered an idiosyncratic interpretation of two iconic, yet radically contrasting, works: Jacob Epstein's *Torso in Metal* from *The Rock Drill* 1913–4 and Barbara Kruger's *Your body is a battleground* 1989. Epstein's *Rock Drill*, belonging to Tate's collection, provided the starting point and formed the basis of the photomontage reproduced in the exhibition leaflet. The sculpture was originally conceived as a full-length plaster figure designed to sit astride a functioning rock drill – an aggressive and hypermasculine symbol of the new machine age – but was bisected and mutated by Epstein in response to the destruction of the First World War before being cast into bronze. 'Here is the sinister figure of today and tomorrow. No humanity, only the terrible Frankenstein's monster we have made ourselves into.'[2]

Davis is drawn to the ambiguous space this powerful image occupies, a fractured vision of the future rooted in a specific moment from the past, looking both forwards and backwards, a humanised machine still open for interrogation. *Your body is a battleground* is characteristic of Kruger's 1980s graphic works, which co-opted the language of advertising in order to provide a feminist critique of media representations of identity and sexuality. By adding the word 'still' to the title, Davis reactivates the phrase, extracting it from the past and perhaps implying an incomplete project.

1. Kate Davis in conversation with Adam Szymczyk, *Nairy Baghramian/Kate Davis*, exh. cat., Kunsthalle Basel, 2006
2. Epstein in *Autobiography*, 1940, p. 56

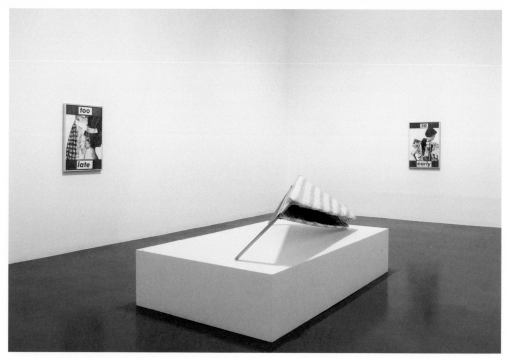

Your body is a battleground still 2007, installation views

Kate Davis 97

The complex interplay between different modes of representation – the pictorial and real, the two-dimensional and three-dimensional, the photographic and the hand-drawn – is central to Davis's practice. Consideration is given to the precise placement of the image or object within the gallery space and the viewer's bodily relationship to each. Thus her installations operate as minimal stage sets through which our passage is carefully orchestrated, encouraging associative connections to ricochet back and forth between each element or gradually, and subtly, accumulate.

A series of thirteen snapshots stretched along the corridor wall leading into the main body of the Art Now space. The majority of the images appeared to depict ambiguous quotidian scenes bearing little connection to one another, abstracted and estranged through close-up crops or their skewed orientation: an arm bent in repose, the viscous contents of a cracked egg, a naked woman easing herself upwards from a bed, a hand supporting fragments of a broken plate over a wooden tabletop. In crude marker pen over each image Davis had drawn the hour, minute and second hands of a clock, a rudimentary means, perhaps, of reinforcing the existence of each photographic moment, embedded in real time and specific place.

The corridor of photographs acted as a prelude to the other elements of the installation. A low plinth positioned at the centre of the space supported a section of mattress and bed frame. The mattress, meticulously cut into a segment the 'shape' of ten minutes as seen on a clock face, was an absurd attempt to give time tangible form. Slumped forlornly on its haunches, its fabric coating stripped away to reveal its intricate internal construction, the bed was still clearly recognisable yet entirely dysfunctional; it was all interior and exterior (one is reminded of the cracked egg), a combination of natural and man-made materials, of hard and soft surfaces.

Pencil-drawn posters adjacent to the sculpture clearly borrowed their format and typography from Kruger, the hard-edged graphics softened through the hand-drawn line. Framed by the words 'too late' and 'so early', Davis's images show the head and torso of a woman with a random jumble of generic domestic

I want to function in the present time (self-portrait II + bricks) 2006

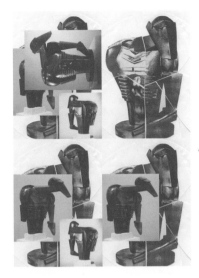

Your body is a battleground still 2007

paraphernalia taped crudely to her person – a plastic spatula, metal whisk, swimming goggles – like redundant armour or prosthetic encumbrances. The images operate as a form of flattened sculptural collage in which the body is treated as sculptural object. In these, Davis seems to be testing out the boundaries of the static image while acknowledging, perhaps, the limitations of Kruger's project; defined by the particular conditions of 1980s consumerism and subsequently criticised for being absorbed by the structures it set out to expose.

Four black and white photographs documenting a systematic action performed by the artist represented a further attempt to symbolise time passing and offered a neat link back to the series of thirteen photographs. In one continuous movement, Davis wrote the word 'still' in marker pen across the centre pages of a sketchbook before removing a page and repeating the action until no pages were left. The word is never shown complete in the images but in a state of perpetual motion, a continual cycle of disappearance and renewal.

In distilling the languages of Epstein and Kruger, Davis reanimates specific moments in history in the present. Time is treated as an indistinct and elastic entity, a structure to be disrupted, as if responding to Yayoi Kusama's claim that 'the consciousness of living in continuation sometimes drives me crazy'. In actively seeking out the fissures and cracks within familiar territories, and dislodging the notion of a 'logical reality'[3], Davis finds alternative spaces in which to operate. Perhaps in this ambiguous space that is neither present, past or future, yet all three at once, new possibilities can be found.

Lizzie Carey-Thomas

3. Kate Davis, op.cit.

The Melancholy of Departure 2006
Courtesy Paul van Esch Collection, The Netherlands

Peter Peri

Peter Peri's paintings and drawings almost seem to inhabit another era; an emerging modern world in the early decades of the last century that now seems more radical, more dangerous, more glamorous. Yet the powerful physical presence of Peri's densely worked and reworked black paintings and time-intensive drawings locates them very much in the 'here and now'. At first sight, the paintings and drawings seem to occupy opposite ends of visual language – the former suggesting the arrangement of form, colour and texture as an end in itself, and the graphic work apparently representing figurative objects or architectural locations. Yet the characteristic that connects these two ongoing bodies of work is a singularly complex handling of space as the viewer is pulled into a seemingly infinite dimension, while at the same time pushed back to the surface of the paint's texture or the detail of pencil line – an action Dan Fox describes as oscillating between the 'microscopic and the macroscopic'.[1]

In *The Melancholy of Departure* 2006 delicate coloured lines delineate triangular black forms that sit in front of, behind or hover alongside each other. The eye is kept moving around and back and forth between these interconnected geometric shapes, carried along by electric-blue, green and pink lines, just as neon light pierces the darkness. As if created by a malfunctioning spider, the grid of this linear network seems to have its own logic while rigorously denying order or pattern. The title refers to a 1914 painting by Giorgio de Chirico, *Gare Montparnasse (The Melancholy of Departure)* which features the symbolic departure of a steam train. It is a scene in which perspective has broken down, signalling a sense of loss but also liberating escape. In the arresting *Country 10* 2006 a loosely painted, pale-green sphere, suggestive of a frail sun or alien moon, is suspended in a roughly drawn cube scratched out of the blackened ground of the canvas. Like Country 10, the fictional location for the radical opera *Victory over the Sun*, first performed in 1913 in St Peterburg with sets and costumes designed by the Russian artist Kasimir Malevich, Peri's painting evokes a bleak futuristic world in which darkness dominates.

Seeking to renew his relationship with figurative imagery, Peri took up drawing just a few years ago, and through drawing came back to painting, continuing to work on both at the same time. Peri comments, 'What does connect them is an equal inclination to disrupt the presence of the form – holes appear in surfaces and edges fade and unravel. There is a simultaneous desire to possess form intimately and to keep it remote, to deliberate obsessively or render it with spontaneity.'[3] The series of drawings titled *The Metropolis and Mental Life* depict tower-like

1. Dan Fox, 'Hairline Fracture', *frieze*, Issue 94, October 2005
2. Kasimir Malevich famously reduced figures and setting to geometric forms which inspired the creation of the modernist icon, *Black Square*, 1915. He wrote in 1927, in *The Non-Objective World*, 'In the year 1913, trying desperately to free art from the dead weight of the real world, I took refuge in the form of the square.' See 'Constructivism' and 'Suprematism' at www.tate.org.uk/collections/glossary for more information
3. All quotations by the artist taken from *Overflow and Extinction*, exh. cat., Counter Gallery, London, 2005

The Metropolis and Mental Life 2006
Courtesy Collection Charles Asprey, London

sculptural forms that appear monumental but give no indication of scale.
Drawn in graphite on Peri's trademark unbleached paper, these angular forms
seem to be made up of organic life forms or tiny hairs that defiantly escape the
imagined outlines of the object depicted. On closer inspection, the falling shadows
ignore perspectival logic and the sides of the structures sit at odds with each
other, disrupting the spatial illusion. *Country of the Blind* 2006 portrays
a three-dimensional structure made up of pyramids and trapezoids reminiscent
of a modernist sculpture presented on a base plinth, or a futuristic city floating
above the ground. Yet any literal reading breaks down as the eye is drawn towards
the inwardly collapsing, murky space at the centre of the image. Peri's depictions
of ornate flower arrangements seem an anomaly amongst the predominance of
abstract and geometric imagery, yet they have their own internal and disorienting
logic. *Le Langage des Fleurs* 2006 is made up of repetitive lines and marks,
creating an effect almost like tapestry. Through the process of peering in closer,
the image dissolves into intricate decorative patterning.

In a famous lecture to art students in 1959 Frank Stella describes 'the two
problems in painting. One is to find out what painting is and the other is to find
out how to make a painting.' He outlines how he approached the first by looking at
and imitating other painters, technically, emotionally and intellectually immersing
himself in their work. 'Fortunately,' Stella continues,' 'I got tired of other peoples'
paintings and began to make my own.'[4] Like Stella, Peri has set about investigating
the legacies of modernist movements, in particular Constructivism and Suprematism,
as a way of finding his own personal set of pictorial codes. A statement by El
Lissitsky offers an insight into the constant play or push and pull between spatial
dimensions that defines Peri's own practice: 'Suprematism has swept away the

4. Frank Stella, *Pratt Institute Lecture*, 1959–60, reproduced in *Art in Theory, 1900–1990*,
edited by Charles Harrison and Paul Wood, Blackwell, 1992, p. 805

Installation view
Courtesy the artist and Counter Gallery, London

illusion of three-dimensional space on a plane, replacing it by the ultimate illusion of *irrational* space with attributes of infinite extensibility of depth and foreground.'[5] Peri describes his engagement in these earlier artistic and political systems as 'an engagement with coded systems that manage to divorce themselves from the objective world, and in particular the discovery within those systems of the pursuit of a synthetic universe.'

Peri's paintings and drawings continually disrupt and disorient, compelling the viewer to keep looking, searching for a way to possess the work. The interdependent parts of each carefully constructed composition cannot be isolated, but are held in exquisitely balanced tension by the treatment of the image as one holistic composite. As Peri comments, 'I think this is one of the most powerful things you can get from looking at paintings, that sudden perception of things as utterly precarious, where everything is paradoxically held in place by an overwhelming fullness.'

Katharine Stout

5. El Lissitsky, *A. and Pangeometry*, 1925, ibid. p. 305

Head 5 2006
Courtesy Private Collection, Basel

Unfriendly Game 2006
Courtesy the Zabludowicz Art Trust

Sculpture Court

Lightbox

Live

Enrico David
Chicken Man Gong

Drawing is the starting point for most of my work, from the rendering of
a photographic image to a more intuitive, spontaneous approach. I often
borrow from traditional craft techniques and design styles, using their pre-
given rules and functional potential in an attempt to organise and give structure
to the often chaotic nature of my emotional response to reality. In so doing,
my work often manifests itself in installation-based displays where the
suggestion of a narrative provides a backbone to the arrangement of objects
and images which might be manufactured in a variety of ways.

Both in its physical and acoustic properties, *Chicken Man Gong* is intended
as a visualisation of distress, the clarity (or lack of it) through which a language
strives to communicate, and often fails.

If it refers to the canons of institutional critique, it is only consequential
to my interest in investigating the relationship between expectations and
outcomes, demands and their encounter with the world, and setting up
the cycle work/ curator/museum as a form of psychodrama, a role play.
In view of this, the vitrine is only a partial 'acting out' of device aimed at the
comprehension (or lack of it) of the work. The piece as a whole intends to be
an interruption to the steps we take towards a deeper understanding and a surer
grasp upon things. It is partly a parody, but it also performs as a model, an area
of conflict through which one element makes itself available to perform/be
performed in its ritualistic function. The artwork as an object to be hit, to take
the blows, voicing a demand and testing the language through which that
demand is posed. The gong will be struck according to no particular order of
events. Existing and being installed for the duration of the show is all that is
needed to know.

Enrico David

Italian-born Enrico David has lived and worked in London since the early 1990s.
He produces sculpture, painting and installations that are usually generated from
the practice of drawing, manifesting a tension between schematic two- and
sculptural three-dimensionality. David's body of work to date shows a complex
and constantly evolving personal culture of aesthetics. He mines a number of
visual sources aside from 'fine art' in order to test art's place in the world as it is
filtered through its many associated visual languages: from folk craft to modernist
design to corporate graphic display. His configurations of images and objects
often invite the viewer into a fictional tableau, dramatising the encounter with
the artwork as though it were a piece of theatre.

Opposite: *Chicken Man Gong* (detail) 2005, installation view, Tate Britain Sculpture Court
All works courtesy the artist and Cabinet Gallery, London

Chicken Man Gong 2005, installation views

Spring Session Men 2003
Courtesy the artist and Project
Art Centre, Dublin

In many of his works, David creates forms of figurative sculpture or drawing that 'stand in' for his own presence. In the Art Deco-influenced mise-en-scène titled *Madreperlage* at Cabinet Gallery, London in 2003, David set an oversized rag doll slumped against one of the dark wooden pieces of furniture. The doll's exaggerated scale, lumpy body and ungainly posture sat uncomfortably – both literally and metaphorically – amid the sleek interior design. *MANTWAT* at Sadlers Wells in 2004–5 (also presented as a backdrop for Merce Cunningham's dance at the Barbican Centre in 2005) was a giant male figure constructed from plywood as a kind of flat paper doll whose limbs were joined and articulated so as to be able to move in rudimentary ways. *MANTWAT*, like the rag doll, had a macabre, sexually charged quality: drawn lines across his torso appearing like scarification, a lolling red-painted tongue protruding from his mouth. As Amna Malik described it, 'Enrico David attempts to negotiate the contradiction between carnality as subject matter and the carnality of the desiring object, through an attention to a sense of exposure, embarrassment in relation to the body'[1] These out-of-place figures appear in deliberately awkward contrast with David's recurring motif of a fantasy of sameness repeated in a line-drawn train of repeated, corporate everymen joined together to create a decorative frieze, such as those painted on the walls of his striking grey, black and white 'boardroom' installation *Spring Session Men* at Project Art Centre, Dublin in 2003.

For the sculpture court at Tate Britain, David presented two sculptural objects. The central piece, *Chicken Man Gong*, represented a form of public sculpture which doubled as a ritualistic instrument. The hybrid chicken-man-gong figure appeared, and appealed, to the artist as an 'unreasonable' form, teetering on an elegant stockinged foot (taken from a photograph by Pierre Molinier). A number of objects and images, both made and collected by the artist, were displayed in the adjacent vitrine. They represented the kind of informative, didactic sources associated with museum display, mimicking but not fulfilling the way in which artworks are shown alongside educational or explanatory material. Art historian

1. Piece on *Flesh at War With Enigma*, Kunsthalle Basel, 2005, Surrealism papers
www.surrealismcentre.ac.uk/publications/papers/journal3/acrobat_files/Malik_review.pdf

Herbert Read, in attempting to define sculpture's essence, went back to two ancient anthropological forms: the amulet and the monument. The amulet was a personal charm carried to ward off evil, while the monument was a site of commemoration. David's conception of the sculptures for this site brought such ancient ideas of what sculpture is into play with a robust, municipal functionality appropriate to an outdoor public space. David wove a fiction around the piece, describing it in terms of a kind of psychodrama: the creature representing an approximate and temporarily adequate equivalent for the artist's subjectivity, stepping somewhat reluctantly, and yet magnificently, onto this public stage.

The sculpture resembles but does not properly function as a musical instrument; specifically, a gong. The gong was scheduled to be activated by patrols of Tate staff, initiating a violent act against the sculptural figure and drawing attention to it with dissonant sound. In this way, the sculpture was incorporated into the social as well as physical fabric of the museum, attempting to intervene in the museum as a specific and ordered network of relationships, as much as treating it as a physical 'site'. The installation of *Chicken Man Gong* simultaneously mimicked the institutional nature of the sculpture court and its neutral, hard-wearing surface, and uncovered its potential as a site of social ritual. With its educational vitrine and its bold, clean-cut edges – not unlike Tate's branding style – the work tried to blend in and at the same time disrupted expectations with its exoticism.

Catherine Wood

Richard Hughes

Richard Hughes
Keep On Onnin'

Richard Hughes makes intricate illusions that trick the viewer and expose the artifice of their making. His sculptures and installations resemble the aftermath of good times gone sour. Bags of jettisoned old clothes, rising damp, burnt-out hedges, bottles of urine, and dog-end residues – are all used to create elaborate histories. Hughes revisits specific cultural moments, as his practice taps into shared memories and bittersweet feelings often reserved for things past their best.

For the Art Now Sculpture Court, Hughes made *Keep On Onnin'* – a three-dimensional recreation of a lens flare. Lens flares are the visual phenomenon caught on film that is caused when a sharp light shines on the lens. Described by Hughes as 'the ghost that haunts visions of summers past', the lens flare has specific nostalgic connotations. It has especial association with the rose-tinted optimism of the hippie era when lens flares cast a magical light on films such as *Easy Rider* 1969 and *Woodstock* 1970, and were a regular feature of album covers. Their apparition in films and photographs seemed to provide a documentary equivalence to psychedelic experience – as though proof of both heightened perception and the drug-induced visions that were seen. When cine-cameras became affordable in the 1970s, the lens flare became a feature in home movies and for a generation it epitomised the perfect summer's moment caught on film. They occur most frequently at the start and the end of a day when the sun slices low through the sky, the in-between times when the world feels at its most transient.

Hughes' title conflated the lens flare with another trend from the same period that came out of the counterculture comics movement in America. It is a variation on 'Keep On Truckin', a catchphrase coined by cartoonist Robert Crumb in *Zap* comics in 1967. This slogan spawned a thousand imitations and adorned everything from t-shirts to bumper stickers and television sitcoms. The phrase 'Keep On Onnin' appeared in a cartoon Crumb made five years later entitled *Remember 'Keep On Truckin'?* which vented his bitterness at the way his idea was continually co-opted and ripped off. This cartoon was composed of twenty-seven panels in ever-decreasing size, each featuring variations on the theme, and each less faithful to the original and increasingly emptied of meaning. Hughes' title insinuated that his sculpture *Keep On Onnin'* was also a poor equivalent, close to the thing it copied, but not close enough. Rather like, Hughes suggested, a 'pound shop' version of a name brand.

Whereas lens flares are fleeting, intangible accidents only witnessed as images after an event, Hughes' installation was deliberately contrived out of physical objects and designed to last all through the summer. Existing as a copy without an original, Hughes' lens flare offered a kind of enhanced realism provocatively at odds with its subject matter. Constructed out of Perspex which gradually accrued grime,

Opposite: *Keep On Onnin'* 2006, installation view, Tate Britain Sculpture Court
Courtesy the artist

Keep On Onnin' grubbied the ideal that it referred to. It spoke of how everything ages and dirties with time, including the hippy dream now sullied by the passage of several decades.

Keep On Onnin' was necessarily a pragmatic construction. It consisted of a dozen or so tinted hexagons that cunningly made use of building, tree, signpost, bench and gravel to position a shaft of colour that stretched all the way from the roof of the Clore Gallery to the edge of the garden. These hexagons had to be made out of a lightweight Perspex material, more normally used for insulating conservatories, so that they could be suspended from overhead branches without fear of accident and would withstand the winds and rains that the months ahead would bring. They were assaulted by pigeons and school groups and were obscured by foliage as the summer wore on. Whilst the chunky geometry of these hexagons stood up to the Post-modernist architecture of the Clore Gallery, the sunbeam they formed differed drastically in sensibility from the eternal, sublime sunsets of Turner's paintings housed therein. Hughes' installation was best viewed from Millbank roadside where all the hexagons could be seen to line up, glimpsed perhaps by passing cyclists or the passengers on top of a bus, their curiosity piqued as they sped past too fast to take it all in. Within the sculpture court, one could walk between the elements of *Keep On Onnin'* and understand the mechanics of how it was made without necessarily understanding the whole. It was only when the viewer stood in front of the sign explaining the work that *Keep On Onnin'* revealed itself.

This is typical of Hughes' deeply modest installations and sculptures. Many of his works are outstanding simulacra, made so well that they are often mistaken for the real thing, and appearing so unassuming and ordinary that they could easily be disregarded: an almost burnt-out match stick; a teenager's bedroom strewn with the mess from a heavy night's partying; a bag of old rags; lava lamps and rising damp; and a plastic bottle filled with piss left somewhere for someone to find. All of these are skewered to tell a story, suggesting something so strange and fantastical that the curious viewer is caught in their tracks and made to wonder. To wonder why, for instance, the matchstick hasn't gone out, or to marvel that the detritus left over from a party should, from a certain angle, suddenly resemble a pouting, petulant teenage face.

Hughes' art is unashamedly sentimental. His works combine the painstaking skill required in making artefacts that look just like real objects with a far rarer talent – the ability to pinpoint and to tap into the emotional tug inherent in the changing world around us. His works present the viewer with the unglamorous habitats that they grew up with, the embarrassingly all too recent past that manages to be simultaneously naff and meaningful. Twisting what at first seem to be banal objects into unlikely scenarios, Hughes' works often perform adroit cultural commentary. He subtly transforms objects so that they meld vantage points from different historical moments. *After The Summer of Like* 2005, for instance, features a sagging sofa that has been infested by a host of magic mushrooms, thus combines drug culture with its drab legacy: Hughes has tie-dyed the upholstery so that the work embodies both the faded dirtiness of the old and psychedelic tie-dye design. It is dingy and banal – the sort of couch where casualties from taking acid end up washed up.

After the Summer of Like 2005,
installation view, The Modern
Institute, Glasgow
Courtesy The Modern Institute /
Toby Webster Ltd, Glasgow

Crucially, Hughes' sculptures rarely trick their viewers for long, and quickly include them in the tale they are spinning. In doing so, they infuse their viewers and subject matters alike with affection. Like many of his works, *Keep On Onnin'* revealed the means of its making and pointedly turned this to its own advantage. The notion of transformation is crucial to Hughes' practice. What appear at first glance to be found objects and scenarios are actually constructed from scratch, so that the viewer of the work undergoes a moment of realisation when expectation is overturned by humour. Rather than attempt to provide mystic truths, Hughes, works conjure mundane miracles: the pebbles stuck over an ugly lamp post are actually hundreds of tiny smiley faces that the artist has made out of Fimo modelling clay; old piles of clothes that look ready to be thrown away are deliberately swirled together to suggest faces from an album cover; and in *Keep On Onnin'*, visions of light are constructed out of plastic.

Keep On Onnin' 2006, installation views, Tate Britain Sculpture Court
Courtesy the artist

Inventory

The Absence of Myth 2004
Courtesy the artist and The Approach, London

Inventory is a group of artists, writers and theorists, established in 1995. Their aim is to create an 'interdisciplinary space' for engaging with contemporary culture, by developing a range of hybrid activities derived from sociology, art, politics, philosophy, literature and anthropology. Inventory's work includes exhibitions in a range of media, as well as radio broadcasts, lectures, graffiti, urban interventions, performance, film and video pieces. An important part of their work is research-based, as reflected by their journal, *Inventory*.

Inventory continue a tradition of sceptical intellectual investigation initiated by figures such as André Breton and the Surrealists, Guy Debord and the Situationists, philosophers such as Walter Benjamin and Georges Bataille, and the anthropologist Roger Callois. The focus of their activities is the contemporary urban environment; they take their name from Benjamin's assertion that 'the inventory of the streets is inexhaustible.'

Despite its title, *The Absence of Myth* is a film which explores the ubiquity of mythic names in urban life. Inventory draw attention to the way that, in being co-opted for prosaic use in street names and advertising, such figures have been robbed of their mythic qualities and status. Their slow, meditative film therefore posits an 'absence' in society.

Ben Tufnell

Damien Roach

According to no plan 2004
Courtesy the artist and Sies + Höke, Düsseldorf

The allure of the everyday and the overlooked is a recurrent theme in the work of Damien Roach. His interest lies in challenging or altering perception, reworking generic, natural imagery in various media to re-evaluate the prosaic. Although unremarkable in subject matter and often unobtrusive in presentation, his work possesses an indeterminate quality that provokes a double take in the viewer and, after further scrutiny, reveals hidden value.

In his film *According to no plan*, Roach explores an archetypal English forest – a landscape we instantly recognise but simultaneously sense as strange. The unexpected, eerie silence of this lively scene, saturated with hyper-real colour, betrays the woodland setting as unnatural and highlights its deliberate construction.

The swirling panoramic treescape is slowly and meticulously captured in over 700 photographic stills taken with a digital camera, that has been rotated manually through 360 degrees. Roach has then animated this material by computer, overlaying individual shots and manipulating the speed and direction in which the images rotate. The resulting vista slips in and out of focus and fragments our view. Roach's image fluctuates between figuration and abstraction. Through his kaleidoscopic vista the forest landscape is represented as a place of reverie. The tangled pattern and hypnotic rhythm of the spinning tree canopy has a mesmerising appeal and as we become enveloped by this visual daydream we are transported from the everyday towards something magical and extraordinary.

Rachel Tant

Matt Calderwood

Battery 2003

Light 2004

Pole 2000
All works courtesy the artist and David Risley Gallery, London

Matt Calderwood's sculptural installations and video works take the form of controlled experiments. They explore the physical properties of common materials and the effects of the artist's often bemusing actions upon them. Calderwood pushes simple activities to their inevitable conclusion by applying logic and an amateur understanding of physics to a range of scenarios, from he banal to the dangerous. For example, chopping away the rungs of a ladder beneath him as he progressively climbs up.

While the outcome is frequently predictable, revealing a perplexing disparity between effort expended and final reward, there is a palpable tension evident in many of Calderwood's works.

In *Battery* 2003 the artist seemingly places himself at risk of serious injury by burning through the ropes that suspend a large car battery above his hands yet is protected by the ingenuity of his system of pulleys. Nevertheless, filmed in real time and unrehearsed, the shaky relief experienced by the artist at the end of the stunt is directly transferred to the viewer.

A poetic melancholy underscores the slapstick simplicity of Calderwood's work. This may provide a metaphor for the ultimate futility and cyclical nature of human endeavour. Yet he also unearths a heroic beauty in his materials by allowing them to fulfil their potential; a single wine glass reveals a surprising strength by supporting a precariously balanced concrete block. In *Light* 2004 an isolated street lamppost's bulb is unscrewed by the artist, a simple act that at once renders it dysfunctional while drawing attention to the dramatic impact it has on its surrounding environment.

Lizzie Carey-Thomas

Steven Claydon

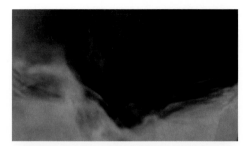

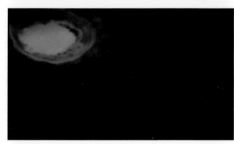

From Earth 2005
Courtesy the artist and HOTEL, London

In *From Earth* we appear to be moving through a mythical spacescape. Amorphous objects drift past and clouds in chemical hues slowly swell and mutate. A milky way is visible and fiery meteorites burn through the viscous atmosphere. The terrain appears unpopulated but a cast of hybrid characters is introduced through the voiceover soundtrack, fantastical creatures with multiple eyes and limbs, from the beautiful to the monstrous.

The descriptive passages have been extracted from the first two chapters of David Attenborough's ambitious account of the evolution of the natural world, *Life on Earth*. Dense with metaphor, the abridgement of Attenborough's text almost enters the realm of poetry as he struggles to summon an image of early forms of life that know no direct equivalent in the modern world. 'Tiers of terraces… rotten eggs… teetering columns and spiky armour… a mat of flailing threads and bulging out fingers… gothic helmets, rococo belfries and spiked space capsules… organ pipes that are blood red.'

The commentary moves beyond the realms of science fiction to suggest a hallucinatory and distorted world, drawing from and merging an infinite pool of natural and man-made references and evoking writers such as Frank Herbert. The visuals appear to be computer-generated but have in fact been compiled from footage filmed by Claydon, in which he never quite settles on any recognisable form. Rooted in the origins of life yet implying an apocalyptic inevitability, Claydon's film seems to reveal an ominous circularity, challenging the notion of a progressive evolution.

Lizzie Carey-Thomas

Craig Mulholland

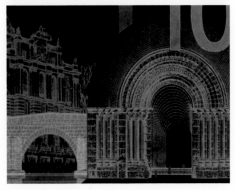

Hyperinflation 2004
Courtesy the artist and Sorcha Dallas, Glasgow

While Craig Mulholland's practice encompasses a range of media, he considers himself primarily a painter and regards his films as a form of 'extended painting'. *Hyperinflation* was first shown as the central element in Mulholland's exhibition *Bearer on Demand*, at Transmission Gallery, Glasgow, 2005: a complex installation that also included sculptures and paintings which addressed the imagery and ideas articulated in the film. The catalyst for the project was a text by William S Burroughs, *Immortality*. Burroughs addresses a vampiric process of 'inconspicuous but inexorable consumption' and concludes: 'The vampire converts quality – live blood, vitality, youth, talent – into quality – food and time for himself. He perpetuates the most basic betrayal of the spirit, reducing all human dreams to his shit.'

Hyperinflation envisages a night-bound Gothic zone in which the vampire serves as a metaphor for money, its role in systems of exchange and its defining position within the structures of capitalist society. This historical analogy has been used by a number of writers and thinkers including Bram Stoker, Franco Moretti and Karl Marx. Marx wrote: 'Capital is dead labour, which, vampire-like, lives only by sucking living labour, and lives the more, the more labour it sucks.'

Hyperinflation was also conceived as a kind of companion piece to Hans Richter's 1927–8 Dadaist film *Inflation,* which addresses runaway inflation in Germany in the early 1920s. Whereas Richter, an influential film pioneer, had limited technical means and used simple montage and collage, Mulholland is able to use sophisticated computer animation technology. His imagery is scanned from coins, old banknotes and his own drawings and paintings, painstaking assembled to create a deliberately ahistorical and ambiguous space. The film itself enacts a vampiric transformation, animating dead and inert matter.

Ben Tufnell

Stephen Sutcliffe

Transformations 2005

Come to the Edge 2003
All works courtesy the artist

Stephen Sutcliffe's two films both take poems as their starting points. *Transformations* is based on the Thomas Hardy poem of he same title. Hardy draws attention to the cycles of death and rebirth that are ever present in the countryside. He describes a man the poet's grandfather knew and his wife, and a 'fair girl', who, in a process of organic renewal, have been transformed into trees and flowers:

> 'They are not underground,
> But as nerves and veins abound
> In the growths of upper air'

Come to the Edge uses a recording of the poet Christopher Logue reciting a poem originally written in 1968:

> 'Come to the edge.
> We might fall.
> Come to the edge.
> It's too high!
> COME TO THE EDGE!
> And they came,
> and we pushed,
> And they flew.'

In the film a good-humoured scene is suddenly transformed into something altogether more sinister as a group of schoolboys enact a ritual humiliation upon a seemingly older, moustachioed boy.

Sutcliffe has an extensive archive of audio and video recordings. In constructing his films he begins with the soundtrack and then, through a process of association, adds imagery to it, sometimes also later adding music. The meshing of soundtrack and visuals is often determined by matching a key moment in each to the other; thus, in *Come To the Edge*, the moment the poet screams the title is aligned to the cry of the boy under attack. However, the relationships Sutcliffe establishes in this way are complex and not simply illustrative. While the imagery in *Transformations* confirms the surreal pastoralism of Hardy's poem, in *Come to the Edge* a profound disjunction between image and soundtrack is created – between Logue's inspirational invocation of risk and the unsettling violence of the film – leading to a profound reassessment of the meaning of both.

Ben Tufnell

Suky Best & Rory Hamilton

Interlude 2005

Train Hold-up 2005

Village Gunfight 2005
All works courtesy the artists and Danielle Arnaud
contemporary art, London

Suky Best and Rory Hamilton's collaborative
animations take archetypal scenes from classic
cowboy movies and remove everything
but the silhouette of the hero (and his horse)
in order to explore his mythic status and the
filmic structures that support this. For the
artists the cowboy represents 'a heroic
symbol, the loner in a world of simple
morality.' Best and Hamilton direct our
attention at certain moments which, despite
the lack of visual information given, are
instantly recognisable as conforming to
narrative conventions of the cowboy genre:
a stranger arriving in town, a gunfight in a bar,
a train hold-up. The original films themselves
are unidentified but nonetheless familiar.

Best and Hamilton's films are
painstakingly hand-animated frame by frame
using a technique called Rotoscoping. In this
technique the original films are turned into
still photographs which are then interpreted
by the animators. The resulting shorts have
a handmade quality which computer
animations cannot achieve.

While interested in exploring the narrative
implications of these fragmentary moments
the artists are also concerned with the
perceptual effects that their technique
produces. The films employ a technique
called 'occlusion' in which figures and objects
are only made visible as the hero passes
behind them. From minimal information
the brain is able to hold and interpret such
imagery and recreate a complete tableau.
Best and Hamilton's work thus enacts a
process of cognitive perception, whereby
the viewer mentally recreates the original
imagery. This process seems to symbolically
suggest that the mythic figure of the hero –
the only figure we actually 'see' – somehow
creates the world around himself as he moves
through it.

Ben Tufnell

Duncan Campbell

o Joan, no... 2006
Courtesy the artist

o Joan, no... begins in darkness; abstract darkness, primordial darkness perhaps. As the film progresses the darkness is interrupted by light or a light. A random sequence of lights ensues – theatre lights, streetlights, household lights, the lit end of a cigarette. The camera greets these interruptions in the darkness with alarm, reticence, perplexity, curiosity. The accompanying voice emits a series of grunts, moans, sighs, laughs. Nothing happens.

Duncan Campbell

Conceived as the first chapter of a longer film, *o Joan, no...* 2006 promises much but never seems to get started. Instead the viewer is privy to darkness and spots of light, to a voice-over in which nothing is said. Duncan Campbell's piece is a homage to the Irish playwright Samuel Beckett, who described his own body of work as 'a stain upon silence'. *o Joan, no...* refers in particular to Beckett's play *Play* 1963, in which darkness is interrupted by a spotlight that picks out each actor in turn. *o Joan, no...* is different from previous works by Campbell, which relied heavily upon found materials. For example, *Falls Burns Malone Fiddles* 2003 presents an overlayering of documentation to affect a disintegration of meaning. Archival footage depicting Belfast during the Troubles of the 1970s and 1980s is disrupted by superimposed graphs, diagrams and drawn black outlines. A voice-over in a near-impenetrable Scottish accent accompanies the images, at times trying and failing to lip-synch to them. In contrast, adrift from any particular time or place, composed entirely from new footage and presenting minimal action or information, *o Joan, no...* seems in many ways the direct opposite to *Falls Burns Malone Fiddles*. However, its images of darkness and nothingness continue Campbell's preoccupations with humanity's oldest themes.

Gair Boase

Declan Clarke

Mine Are of Trouble 2006
Courtesy of the artist

Declan Clarke's video *Mine Are of Trouble* 2006 deftly juxtaposes an account of socialist Rosa Luxemburg's life against his own personal and haphazard introduction to the revolutionary figure whilst he was living in Berlin. The political activist's remarkable actions, which culminated in her assassination in 1919, are set in poignant contrast to Clarke's failed attempts to transfer her political legacy to his own romantic life.

The film takes the form of a documentary but is striking for its personal involvement in its subject as well as for its idiosyncratic approach. It is made up of two very uneven halves. The first tells the story of Rosa Luxemburg through grainy old photographs and hand-held camera footage of Berlin as it is now and also incorporates an impassioned voice-over delivered by Clarke in his lilting Irish accent. The second part of the film unfolds mostly in silence, narrated as inter-titles between still photographs. The subject shifts to Clarke himself, his interest in Luxemburg and his attempts to persuade a succession of girlfriends to name their non-existent daughters Rosa. By linking the incidents of the socialist revolutionary's life to his own meandering biography, Clarke shows the historical figure as a human being. His skill is to weave the personal into the political and vice versa, and to show that the two are inextricably related.

Lizzie Carey-Thomas

Emily Wardill

Born Winged Animals and Honey Gatherers of the Soul 2005

Supported by the Arts Council England. Courtesy Fortescue Avenue / Jonathan Viner, London

Emily Wardill's 16 mm film *Born Winged Animals and Honey Gatherers of the Soul* 2005 is set within earshot of the bells of St Anne's Church designed by Hawksmoor in Limehouse, London, as they strike noon. This work is a mesmerising visual and phonetic study of a symbol cited in *On the Genealogy of Morality* 1887 by nineteenth-century German philosopher Friedrich Nietzsche. In this text he argues that humans have never been able to find out who they really are and even in the attempt to do so they inevitably lose themselves:

> Rather, much as a divinely distracted, self-absorbed person into whose ear the bell has just boomed its twelve strokes of noon suddenly awakens and wonders, 'What did it actually toll just now?' so we rub our ears afterwards and ask, 'What did we actually experience just now?' still more: 'Who are we actually?' and count up afterwards, as stated, all twelve quavering bell strokes of our life, of our being – alas! And miscount in the processes.

The film evokes the poetic mood of Nietzsche's text by alternating between the sonorous rhythm of the bells and recorded snapshots of everyday life in this area of east London. Wardill re-uses symbols, examples and idealistic spaces as her own stages, away from their initial meanings and intents. *Born Winged Animals and Honey Gatherers of the Soul* harnesses the visceral impact of bells tolling, and contrasts this with evocative realist film footage to both suggest and dissolve the symbol that Nietzsche uses to put across an individual's attempt to gain self-awareness.

Katharine Stout

Sue Tompkins

Grease 2006, Performance
Courtesy the artist

Sue Tompkins uses the spoken and written
word – sometimes in combination with music,
found images and other ephemeral material –
delivered in a deceptively simple and direct
fashion. The written word comes first:
she accumulates copious notes over a period
of time then edits and refines them to create
disjointed yet succinct texts to evoke imagery,
emotion and ideas. These eclectic fragments
are presented in the gallery on large creased
sheets of newsprint paper that overwhelm
the small lines of mechanical typewritten text.
Together they recollect personal encounters,
ideas and preoccupations that affect her
daily life.

Tompkins is equally well known for her
spoken word performances. Their rhythm
and style are indebted to her experience of
being in a band, but are also notable for the
starkness of their hypnotising delivery.
Performances such as *Country Grammar* 2003,
More Cola Wars 2004 and *Elephants Galore*
2005 are read from up to 300 pages worth
of notes: while some pages might contain
one word others might have many.

Made up of text that is original, altered
or borrowed from songs, writings or
conversations, the strength of Tompkins' work
is in its disruption of verbal communication.
Through complex yet eloquent layerings
of repetition, odd and non-sequential
juxtaposition and a re-contextualisation
of words, Tompkins reinvigorates and gives
new meaning to language. Her new work
Grease 2006, written over eight months,
was presented for the first time at Tate Britain.

Katharine Stout

The Mare's Nest; a History of Provenance 2006, performance
Courtesy the artist

Rory Macbeth

In *The Mare's-Nest: A History of Provenance* Rory Macbeth presented a series of tours of cherished works at Tate Britain posing as a tour guide. His histories of the works, presented in a formal and academic style, were entirely fictitious, including a discussion of a Constable whose composition is based on the London Tube map, a Turner that has become a shrine to Marc Bolan, and a Sutherland which is hung as a landscape and a portrait on alternate weeks, since no one knows which way up it goes.

Rory Macbeth works in a wide variety of media, encompassing tromp l'oeil waxworks, graffiti, performance and hearsay. His practice probes the gap between ideals and their realization, between what is presented to us and what we actually get. It is the effort to uphold the ideal in the face of reality that Macbeth is interested in; in the tragicomedy of the pretence that ensues. In the past, Macbeth has sculpted trees from wood and rocks from stone. While studying at Central St Martins College, he and a fellow classmate Laura Lord exploited rumour and the college administration to create a fake student who gained a distinction. His meticulously crafted waxworks of buskers pretending to be sculptures on the street earned up to £25 an hour, from appreciative passers-by. A recent project saw the entirety of Sir Thomas More's humanist text *Utopia* which outlines his reflections upon an ideal society, written as graffiti around the outside of a building due to be demolished.

Macbeth recently undertook a follow-up tour at Tate Britain, *The Doppleganger Shift: The Art-copy and Deceipt*, in which he claimed that all the major works in the Tate and the National Gallery were copied as part of the Second World War effort to preserve the nation's treasures, and these replaced the originals which were kept for safety in a Welsh mine.

Gair Boase

Joanne Tatham & Tom O'Sullivan

Think, Think Thingamajig; what do you represent?
2006
Courtesy the artists

Joanne Tatham and Tom O'Sullivan have worked collaboratively since 1995 making enigmatic images, sculptural objects and installations. The objects regularly resemble esoteric props from an avant-garde play and are designed to inhabit a range of scenarios, from gallery space to public park. They activate their surroundings and cajole the viewer into participating in an absurd kind of theatre.

While a host of identifiable cultural and art historical references are embedded in the works, deciphering their origins offers no greater insight into meaning. Presented with a series of cul-de-sacs and double-backs, we are forced instead to contemplate the artwork as a thing on its own terms, as an event or encounter in real time and space. This process is facilitated by the banality and absurdity of the forms which nevertheless dramatise the space and confront the viewer in all their physicality.

Tatham and O'Sullivan regularly re-stage and rework imagery and objects from their practice in a variety of different formats, reducing them to a vocabulary of simplified symbols or motifs. *Think, Think Thingamajig; what do you represent?*, their new work for Art Now, was a live recreation of one in a series of drawings in which sculptural objects interact with top-hatted, be-suited figures. These figures have also featured in photographic works and sculptural tableaux (often as crude stick men) and function as an emblem for both artist and audience. In the drawing *Think, Think Thingamajig, think* 2005, the Think Thingamajig – a cube decorated with pink diamonds against a black background which first appeared as a ceramic sculpture in 2003 – becomes a costume sported by a gentleman who sits slumped in thoughtful contemplation. By translating the scene into a piece of living sculpture in the gallery Tatham and O'Sullivan enabled image, object and event to coalesce.

Lizzie Carey-Thomas

Artists' biographies
Lists of works

Jananne Al-Ani

Born in Kirkuk, Iraq, 1966
Lives and works in London

1995–7   MA Photography, Royal College of Art,
          London

Selected solo exhibitions

2005   *The Visit*, Art Now, Tate Britain, London
2004   *The Visit*, Norwich Gallery
2002   Dryphoto Art Contemporanea, Prato
        Les Rencontres de la Photographie,
        Musée Reattu, Arles

Selected group exhibitions

2007   *The Screen-Eye or the New Image: 100 videos
        to rethink the world*, Casino Luxembourg
2006   *Why Pictures Now: Photography, Film and
        Video Today*, Museum Moderner Kunst,
        Vienna
        *Without Boundaries: Seventeen Ways of
        Looking*, Museum of Modern Art, New York
2005   *The World is a Stage: Stories Behind Pictures*,
        Mori Art Museum, Tokyo
        Identità & Nomadismo, Palazzo delle
        Papesse, Siena

Curated exhibitions

2003–4 *Veil*, The New Art Gallery Walsall, touring
        to Bluecoat Arts Centre and Open Eye
        Gallery, Liverpool; Modern Art Oxford
        and Kulturhuset, Stockholm
2001–2 *Fair Play*, Danielle Arnaud contemporary
        art, London, touring to Angel Row Gallery,
        Nottingham

Exhibited work

The Visit
A work in two parts:

Muse 2004
16 mm film transferred to DVD, 15 min
Single channel projection, 190 × 300 cm

Echo 1994–2004
VHS transferred to DVD, 10 min
Four channel projection, 30 × 30 cm each

Courtesy the artist and Union, London
Commissioned by Film and Video Umbrella and
Norwich Gallery. Supported by Arts Council England,
Film London and the Henry Moore Foundation

Suky Best

Born in London, 1962
Lives and works in London

1992–5   MA Photography, Royal College of Art,
          London

Selected solo exhibitions

2008   *Rodeo*, Danielle Arnaud contemporary art,
        London
2005   *Return of the Native*, Film and Video
        Umbrella Commission, BCA Gallery
        Bedford and Pump House Gallery, London
        Wild West (with Rory Hamilton), Art Now
        Lightbox, Tate Britain, London and Danielle
        Arnaud contemporary art, London

Selected group exhibitions

2007   *Towards a New Ease*, Fotomuseum
        Winterthur, Switzerland
        Scodown!, D.U.M.B.O. Arts Center,
        New York
2006   *Timeless:time, landscape and new media*,
        Harbourfront Center, Toronto, Canada
        MIMA:offsite, Middlesbrough Institute
        of Modern Art
2005   *Exhumed*, Museum of Garden History,
        London
2003   *East International*, Norwich Gallery, Norwich

Commissions

2007   Great North Run, Moving Image Commission
        Sculpture in Woodland Commission, Devil's
        Glen, Ireland
        Permanent video projection, Main Reception,
        University College Hospital, London

Exhibited work

Village Gunfight 2005
DVD, 2 min 29 sec

Stranger in Town 2005
DVD, 1 min 46 sec

Interlude 2005
DVD, 1 min 19 sec

Train Hold-up 2005
DVD, 1 min 29 sec

All works courtesy the artists and Danielle Arnaud
contemporary art, London

Matt Calderwood

Born in Northern Ireland, 1975
Lives and works in London

1994–7 BA Hons Fine Art, Sunderland University, England
1993–4 Foundation Art and Design, Newcastle College

Selected solo exhibitions

2007 David Risley Gallery, London
Canon's Marsh / Bristol Harbourside, Bristol
Hot Air, Taxter and Spengemann, New York
2005 *DIM,* David Risley Gallery, London

Selected group exhibitions

2007 *Discovering Slowness,* KW14
's-Hertogenbosch, touring to the National Centre of Photography, Saint Petersburg
Matt Calderwood, Marine Hugonnier, Corey McCorkle, Project 88, Mumbai
2006 *Geladen: Videokunst (screening),* Museum Ludwig, Cologne
Kaleidoscope (screening), Whitechapel Art Gallery, London
Risk & Allure, Haus Für Kunst Uri, Altdorf
Pick Your Poison, Galerie Martin Van Zomeren, Amsterdam
Mythkillers, Galleria Klerkx, Milan
Sounds Of Silence, Galerie Gisela Capitain, Cologne
2005 *Freezer,* Archeus, London
De Nachten, deSingel, Antwerp
Art Now Lightbox, Tate Britain, London

Exhibited work

Pole 2000
DVD, 1 min 30 sec

Battery 2003
DVD, 2 min 2 sec

Light 2004
DVD, 47 sec

All works courtesy the artist and David Risley Gallery, London

Duncan Campbell

Born in 1972
Lives and works in Glasgow

Selected solo exhibitions

2006 *The Unnamable,* Lux at Lounge, London
2005 *Something in Nothing,* TART Contemporary, San Francisco
2004 *Falls Burns Malone Fiddles,* Galerie Luis Campaña, Cologne
2003 *Falls Burns Malone Fiddles,* Transmission Gallery, Glasgow

Selected group exhibitions

2006 Art Now Lightbox, Tate Britain, London
Archaeology of Today?, The Kosova Art Gallery, Prishtina
Ein Zentrum in der Peripherie, Galerie Peripherie, Sudhaus, Tübingen
2005 *Art From Glasgow,* Temple Bar Gallery, Dublin
The Need to Document, Halle für Kunst, Lueneburg
2004 *Manifesta 5,* European Biennial of Contemporary Art, San Sebastian

Exhibited work

o Joan, no... 2006
16mm film transferred onto DVD
Courtesy the artist

Declan Clarke

Born in 1974
Lives and works in London

1999–2000	MA Fine Art, Chelsea College of Art & Design, London
1995–7	BA Hons Fine Art, National College of Art & Design, Dublin

Selected solo exhibitions

2007	*Rebellion and Plots Ripen Like Fruit*, Kiosko, Santa Cruz, Bolivia
2006	*Trauma and Romance*, Gallery 3 Off-site project at The Shaw Birthplace, Douglas Hyde Gallery, Dublin
	Mine Are of Trouble, Four Gallery, Dublin

Selected group exhibitions

2007	*Left Pop*, Moscow Museum of Modern Art, Moscow Biennale, Moscow
2006	*Enthusiasm*, Frieze Projects, Frieze Art Fair, London
	To Hell with Dixie, Galerie Groeflin Maag, Basel
	Art Now Lightbox, Tate Britain, London
2005	*Encounters with the Subordinary*, Hornsey Pumphouse, London
	Communism, Project, Dublin
2003	*International Residency Programme*, P.S.1 Contemporary Art Center, New York
2002	*The Friendship of the Peoples (Goshka Macuga and Declan Clarke)*, Project, Dublin

Exhibited work

Mine Are Of Trouble 2005
Video transferred onto DVD
15 min 50 sec
Courtesy the artist

Steven Claydon

Born in 1969
Lives and works in London

1997	MA Fine Art, Central Saint Martins School of Art & Design, London
1991	BA Hons Fine Art: Painting, Chelsea College of Art & Design, London

Selected solo exhibitions

2007	*New Valkonia*, David Kordansky, Los Angeles
2006	*Courtesy of the Neighbourhood Watch*, White Columns, New York
2005	*All Across the Thready Eye*, Galerie Dennis Kimmerich, Düsseldorf
	Fear of a Planet, HOTEL, London

Selected group exhibitions

2007	*Old School,* Hauser and Wirth Colnaghi, London, travelling to Zwirner and Wirth, New York
	Pale Carnage, Arnolfini, Bristol
	Come Into The Open, Opening Exhibition Projekt 0047, Oslo
2006	*The Metal Bridge*, Sorcha Dallas, Glasgow
	Rings of Saturn, Tate Modern, London
	Keep passing the open window, Galerie Gisela Capitain, Cologne
	Dereconstruction, Barbara Gladstone Gallery, New York,
2005	*Paris – Londres: Le Voyage Interieur*, Espace Electra, Paris
	Even a Stopped Clock Tells the Right Time Twice a Day, Institute of Contemporary Arts, London
	Art Now Lightbox, Tate Britain, London

Exhibited work

From Earth 2005
Video transferred to DVD
4 min 27 sec
Courtesy the artist and HOTEL, London

Enrico David

Born in Italy, 1966
Lives and works in London

1991–4 BA Fine Art, Central Saint Martins College
of Art and Design, London
1990–1 Lina Garnade Foundation Course, London

Selected solo exhibitions

2007 Institute of Contemporary Art, London
Shitty Tantrum, Cabinet, London
Stedelijk Museum, Amsterdam
2005 *Chicken Man Gong*, Art Now Sculpture
Court commission, Tate Britain, London
Galerie Daniel Buchholz, Cologne
Wizard's Sleeve, Cabinet, London
2004 *Douche That Dwarf*, Transmission, Glasgow

Selected group exhibitions

2007 *Door Slamming Festival*, Links, Berlin
2006 *GIRLPOWER AND BOYHOOD*,
Talbot Rice Gallery, Edinburgh
Kunsthallen Brandts Klaedefabrik, Odense
How to Improve the World, 60 years of
British Art, Arts Council Collection,
Hayward Gallery, London
Tate Triennial, Tate Britain, London
Galerie Buchholz at Metro Pictures,
New York
The Subversive Charm of the Borgeoisie,
Van Abbemuseum, Eindoven
2005 *British Art Show 6*,
Hayward Gallery national touring
exhibition
Monuments for the USA, CCA Wattis,
Institute for Contemporary Arts,
San Francisco (travelling to White Columns,
New York)
Suave Deat, Triangle Arts, Havana
2004 *Vernice. Sentieri della
giovane pittura italiana*, Villa Manin
2003 *Dreams and Conflicts: The Dictatorship of
the Viewer*, Venice Biennale

Exhibited work

Chicken Man Gong 2005
Mixed media
Dimensions variable
Courtesy the artist and Cabinet Gallery, London

Kate Davis

Born in New Zealand, 1977
Lives and works in Glasgow

2000–1 MPhil Art & Design in
Organisational Contexts, Glasgow School
of Art, Glasgow
1997– BA Hons Fine Art,
2000 Glasgow School of Art, Glasgow

Selected solo exhibitions

2007 *Your body is a battleground still*, Art Now,
Tate Britain, London
Waiting in 1972; what about 2007?, solo
statement with Sorcha Dallas, Art Basel
2006 *STOP! STOP! STOP!,* Kunsthalle Basel, Basel
I want to function in the present time,
Art Forum Berlin with Sorcha Dallas
Build Cracks, Dicksmith Gallery, London
2005 *Could we? I am asking*, The Breeder, Athens

Selected group exhibitions

2006 *If I can't dance I don't want to be part of your
revolution*, De Appel, Amsterdam
Summer Show 2006, Anna Helwing Gallery,
Los Angeles
2005 *The Music of the Future*, Gasworks Gallery,
London
Exile: New York is a Good Hotel, Broadway
1602, New York

Exhibited work

Your body is a battleground still (bed) 2007
Mixed media
250 × 180 × 40 cm

Your body is a battleground still (photo series 1–13)
2007
Colour and black and white photographs
24 × 15 × 3 cm (framed)

Your body is a battleground still (poster series 1–3) 2007
Pencil on paper
100 × 75 × 10 cm (framed)

Your body is a battleground still (still series) 2007
Black and white photographs
16 × 24 × 3 cm (framed)

All works courtesy the artist and Sorcha Dallas,
Glasgow

Michael Fullerton

Born in Bellshill, 1971
Lives and works in Glasgow and London

2000–2   MA, Glasgow School of Art, Glasgow

Selected solo exhibitions

2006   Greene Naftali Gallery, New York
2005   *Suck on Science*, Art Now, Tate Britain,
        London
        Suck on Science, CCA, Glasgow
2003   *Are You Hung Up?*, Transmission Gallery,
        Glasgow, Counter Gallery, London and
        Generator Projects, Dundee

Selected group exhibitions

2006   *Toutes Compositions Florales*, Counter
        Gallery
        This is not a painting, The Open Eye Club
        at The Glasgow Project Room
        Tate Triennial, Tate Britain, London
2004   *Quodlibet*, Galerie Daniel Buchholz,
        Cologne
        Wider than the Sky, 117 Commercial Street,
        London
2003   *Bloomberg New Contemporaries*,
        Cornerhouse, Manchester and
        14 Wharf Road, London
        Prague Biennale, Prague, Czech Republic

Exhibited work

*A Loyal Beautiful Aesthete for a World That Didn't
Care* 2005
Oil on canvas
60 × 45 cm

Ross McWhirter Aged 13 at the Outbreak of the War
2004
Oil on linen
60 × 45 cm
The Cranford Foundation, London

Untitled 2004
Paper, mirror, Ferric oxide
30 × 60 cm

Cones 2005
Reworked illustration from *Ocular Anatomy
and Histology*
Ferric oxide, urethane, microphone
Dimensions variable

David Milligan 2005
Oil on canvas
90 × 70 cm

John Peel 2005
Oil on canvas
180 × 100 cm

Silence is So Accurate 2005
Newsprint bale
Dimensions variable

*Who Keeps the World Both Old and New, in Pain
or Pleasure?* 2005
Reworked illustration from *Ocular Anatomy
and Histology*
Mild Steel, BASF variochrome
Dimensions variable

Nietzsche's House in Panascope
2005
Silk-screen prints on newsprint
Dimensions variable

Untitled 2005
DVD
Dimension variable

Unless otherwise stated all works courtesy the
artist and Counter gallery, London

Andrew Grassie

Born in Edinburgh, 1966
Lives and works in London

1988–90   MA Painting, Royal College of Art, London
1984–8   BA Hons Fine Art Painting, Central Saint
          Martin's School of Art and Design, London

Selected solo exhibitions

2008   Talbot Rice Gallery, Edinburgh
2006   *Installation*, Maureen Paley, London
       Private, Sperone Westwater, New York
2005   *New Hang*, Art Now, Tate Britain, London
2003   *Group Show*, Mobile Home Gallery,
       London

Selected group exhibitions

2007   *Very Abstract and Hyper Figurative*,
       Thomas Dane Gallery, London
2006   *The Studio*, Hugh Lane Gallery, Dublin
       Wrong, Galerie Klosterfelde, Berlin
2005   *In search of the real George Eliot*, Hatton
       Gallery, Newcastle
       News from Nowhere, Lucy Mackintosh,
       Lausanne

Exhibited work

New Hang 1 2005
Tempera on paper
15 × 23 cm
Courtesy the artist and Maureen Paley, London

New Hang 2 2005
Tempera on paper
15 × 23 cm
Private collection, courtesy Jeremy Lewison Ltd

New Hang 3 2005
Tempera on paper
15 × 23 cm
Collection of Michael Sandler and Brenda
Potter-Sandler, Los Angeles

New Hang 4 2005
Tempera on paper
15 × 23 cm
Collection of Mickey Cartin, Connecticut

New Hang 5 2005
Tempera on paper
15 × 23 cm
Courtesy the artist and Maureen Paley, London

New Hang 6 2005
Tempera on paper
15 × 23 cm
Courtesy the artist and Maureen Paley, London

New Hang 7 2005
Tempera on paper
15 × 23 cm
Courtesy the artist and Maureen Paley, London

New Hang 8 2005
Tempera on paper
25.9 × 33.6 cm
Collection of Mickey Cartin, Connecticut

New Hang 9 2005
Tempera on paper
15 × 23 cm
Courtesy the artist and Maureen Paley, London

New Hang 10 2005
Tempera on paper
15 × 23 cm
Collection of Anthony Terrana, Massachusetts

New Hang 11 2005
Tempera on paper
15 × 23 cm
Courtesy the artist and Maureen Paley, London

New Hang 12 2005
Tempera on paper
15 × 23 cm
Collection of Chong H. Tay, London

New Hang 13 2005
Tempera on paper
15 × 23 cm
Collection of Ealan Wingate, New York

Rory Hamilton

Born in 1967
Lives and works in London

Selected solo exhibitions

2008   *Rodeo*, Danielle Arnaud contemporary art,
        London
2005   Art Now Lightbox, Tate Britain, London
        Wild West (with Suky Best), Danielle
        Arnaud contemporary art, London
2003   *Arts Centre Nabi* (with Jon Rogers), Korea
        The Brunswick Project, London
2002   *Generic Sci-Fi Quarry* (with Jon Rogers)

Exhibited work

Village Gunfight 2005
DVD, 2 min 29 sec

Stranger in Town 2005
DVD, 1 min 46 sec

Interlude 2005
DVD, 1 min 19 sec

Train Hold-up 2005
DVD, 1 min 29 sec

All works courtesy the artists and Danielle Arnaud
contemporary art, London

Richard Hughes

Born in Birmingham, 1974
Lives and works in London

2001–3   Goldsmiths College, University of London
1992–5   Staffordshire University, England

Selected solo exhibitions

2006   *Keep On Onnin'*, Art Now Sculpture Court
        commission, Tate Britain, London
2005   *What a Dude'll Do*, Nils Staerk,
        Copenhagen
        The Modern Institute, Glasgow
2004   Roma Roma Roma, Rome

Selected group exhibitions

2006   *Among the ash heaps and millionaires*,
        Ancient & Modern, London
        *If it didn't exist you'd have to invent it:
        a partial Showroom history*, The Showroom,
        London
        Becks Futures 2006, Institute of
        Contemporary Arts, London and tour
2005   *British Art Show 6*, Hayward Gallery
        national touring exhibition
        The Addiction, Gagosian Gallery, Berlin
        Bridge Freezes Before Road, Gladstone
        Gallery, New York
        Ordering the Ordinary, Timothy Taylor
        Gallery, London
        Drawing 200, The Drawing Room,
        Tannery Arts, London

Exhibited work

Keep On Onnin' 2005
Mixed media
Dimensions variable
Courtesy the artist

Inventory

Established 1995
Lives and works in London
and Toulouse

Selected solo exhibitions

2004   The Approach, London
Things You Don't Know, Galerie K&S Berlin
and Home Gallery, Prague
Exhibition No. 12, 6 Portikus, Frankfurt

Selected group exhibitions

2005   Art Now Lightbox, Tate Britain, London
2004   *Re: Presentations of Everyday Life,*
The Approach, London
Inventory, The British Council & Inventory,
Trafo, Budapest
2001   *Century City,* Tate Modern, London
2000   *Protest and Survive,* Whitechapel Art
Gallery, London

Exhibited work

The Absence of Myth 2004
DVD, 5 min 33 sec
Courtesy the artists and The Approach, London

Rory Macbeth

Born in London, 1965
Lives and works in London

Rory Macbeth is part of the Boxing Club collective
based at Limehouse Town Hall, and is co-founder
of PILOT, an ongoing archive and forum for artists
and curators

Selected solo exhibitions

2004   *Oktopia,* VTO Gallery, London
2003   *Thank You,* the Economist Plaza, London
2002   *einzweiBriannien,* (with D. Phizacklea)
Nylon Gallery, London

Selected group exhibitions

2006   *EAST International,* Norwich Gallery,
Norwich
Ego-mania, Galleria Civica de Modena,
Modena
2005   *Co-operative Society,* Northern Gallery
for Contemporary Art, Sunderland
Expanded Painting, Prague Biennale, Prague

Exhibited work

The Mare's Nest: A History of Provenance 2006
Performance
Courtesy the artist

Craig Mulholland

Born in Glasgow, 1969
Lives and works in Glasgow

1987–91   BA Hons Fine Art, Glasgow School of Arts

Selected solo exhibitions

2005   Whitechapel Project Space, Whitechapel Art
          Gallery, London
          Bearer on Demand, Transmission Gallery,
          Glasgow
2003   *Plastic Casino*, Sorcha Dallas, Glasgow

Selected group exhibitions

2006   *The Metal Bridge*, Sorcha Dallas, Glasgow
          If Not Now, Broadway 1602, New York
          BASTARDS, Whitechapel Project Space,
          London
2005   Off-site Project, Glasgow International
          Festival
          Art Now Lightbox, Tate Britain, London

Exhibited work

Hyperinflation 2004
DVD, 4 min
Courtesy the artist and Sorcha Dallas, Glasgow

Silke Otto-Knapp

Born in Germany, 1970
Lives and works in London

1992–7   Degree in Cultural Studies, University
         of Hildesheim
1995–6   MA Fine Arts, Chelsea College of Art &
         Design, London

Selected solo exhibitions

2006   *Love in a Void* (with Jutta Koether),
       Academy of Fine Arts, Vienna
       *Standing Anywhere in the Space in a
       Relaxed Position,* Taka Ishii Gallery, Tokyo
       Figures and Groups, Gavin Brown's
       Enterprise, New York
2005   *soft Queenie,* Art Now, Tate Britain,
       London
2004   greengrassi, London
2003   *25th Floor,* Galerie Daniel Buchholz,
       Cologne
       Orange View, Kunstverein für die
       Rheinlande und Westfalen, Düsseldorf

Selected group exhibitions

2006   *Never For Money, Always For Love,*
       Grazer Kunstverein, Graz
       The Subversive Charm of the Bourgeoisie,
       Van Abbemuseum, Eindhoven
2005   *British Art Show 6,* Hayward Gallery
       national touring exhibition
       Istanbul, 9th International Istanbul
       Biennale, Istanbul
       Thinking of the Outside, Situations, Bristol
2004   *The Undiscovered Country,* Hammer
       Museum, Los Angeles

Exhibited work

soft queenie 2005
Watercolour and gouache on canvas
61 × 40.5 cm

At the brides; the braid 2005
Watercolour and gouache on canvas
81 × 66 cm
Collection of Rachel and Carl Berg, New York

Figure and group 2005
Watercolour and gouache on canvas
126 × 152 cm

Figure (silver) 2005
Watercolour and gouache on canvas
81 × 66 cm
Collection of Martin and Rebecca Eisenberg

Portrait 2005
Watercolour and gouache on canvas
35.5 × 25.5 cm

The bride's chamber scene 2005
Watercolour and gouache on canvas
101 × 101 cm

Two figures facing 2005
Watercolour and gouache on canvas
101 × 76 cm

Woman in boots 2005
Watercolour and gouache on canvas
30 × 60 cm

Unless otherwise stated all works courtesy greengrassi,
London, and Galerie Daniel Buchholz, Cologne

Peter Peri

Born in London, 1971
Lives and works in London

2002–3 MA Fine Art, Chelsea College of Art
        and Design, London

Selected solo exhibitions

2007   Art Now, Tate Britain, London
       Hole Here, Galerie Giti Nourbakhsch,
       Berlin
2006   *Country 10*, Kunsthalle Basel, Basel
2005   *Overflow and Extinction*, Counter Gallery,
       London
2004   *The Grey Point*, Counter Gallery, London

Selected group exhibitions

2006   *How to Improve the World, 60 years of
       British Art,* Arts Council Collection,
       Hayward Gallery, London
       Motion on Paper, Ben Brown Fine Art,
       London
       Toutes Compositions Florales, Counter
       Gallery, London
2005   *Violet from Mother's Grave*, Emily Tsingou
       Gallery, London
       We Disagree, Andrew Kreps Gallery &
       Wrong Gallery, New York
2004   *Death & Magic*, Keith Talent Gallery,
       London
       East End Academy, Whitechapel Art
       Gallery, London
2003   *Bloomberg New Contemporaries*,
       Cornerhouse, Manchester &
       14 Wharf Road, London

Exhibited work

Country 10 2006
Mixed media on canvas
122 × 91 cm
Courtesy of the artist and Counter gallery, London

Head 4 2006
Graphite on unbleached paper
32 × 27 cm
Private Collection

Head 5 2006
Graphite on unbleached paper
43 × 37 cm
Private Collection, Basel

Head Hunter 2006
Mixed media on canvas
152 × 122 cm
Courtesy of the artist and Counter gallery, London

Kaisersaschern 2006
Mixed media on canvas
190 × 160 cm
Courtesy of The Greatford Estates Collection

Le Langage des Fleurs 2006
Graphite on unbleached paper
47.5 × 47.5 cm
Private Collection, Michael and Fiona King, London

Metropolis and Mental Life 2006
Graphite on unbleached paper
62 × 74 cm
Collection Charles Asprey

Night Owl 2006
Mixed media on canvas
123 × 92 cm
Peter Handschin, Switzerland

Soft System 2006
Mixed media on canvas
152 × 122 cm
Courtesy Anne Bransten

The Melancholy of Departure 2006
Mixed media on canvas
152 × 122 cm
Courtesy Paul van Esch collection, The Netherlands

Unfriendly Game 2006
Mixed media on canvas
190 × 150 cm
Courtesy the Zabludowicz Art Trust

Damien Roach

Born in Bromley, 1980
Lives and works in London

2001–3   MA Painting, Royal College of Art, London
1998–   BA Hons Fine Art, Middlesex University,
2001   London

Selected solo exhibitions

2007   *Alexandre da Cunha / Damien Roach*,
       Neuer Aachener Kunstverein, Aachen
2006   *Quanta (Frieze 005)*, Neue Kunst Halle,
       St. Gallen
       Departures, T293, Naples
       The deepness of puddles, Gasworks, London
2005   *Damien Roach*, Sies + Höke, Düsseldorf
       The other day, yesterday, today, tomorrow,
       Schnittraum, Cologne

Selected group exhibitions

2007   *Learn to Read*, Tate Modern, London
       Jerwood Contemporary Painters, Jerwood
       Space, London
2006   *HOUSEWARMING*, Swiss Institute,
       New York
2006   *The Square Root of Drawing*, Temple Bar
       Gallery, Dublin
       *You'll Never Know: Drawing and Random
       Interference*, Hayward Gallery Touring
       Landscape, pl. (-s), Witte Zaal, Ghent
2005   *Ordering the Ordinary*, Timothy Taylor
       Gallery, London
       Art Now Lightbox, Tate Britain, London;
       *Centre of Attention/ Swansong, Always
       a Little Further*, Arsenale, 51st Venice
       Biennale

Exhibited work

According to no plan 2004
DVD, 5 min 48 sec (loop)
Courtesy the artist and Sies + Höke, Düsseldorf

Jimmy Robert

Born in France, 1975
Lives and works in Brussels

2004–5   Rijksakademie of Visual Arts, Amsterdam
1996–9   BA Hons Fine Art and Critical Theory,
         Goldsmiths College, University of London

Selected solo exhibitions

2007   *Art Statements*, Art Basel
2006   *White Light*, Düsseldorf Collective Gallery
       (black box), Edinburgh
       Instabilly, Diana Stigter, Amsterdam
       6 things we couldn't do, but can do now,
       Art Now, Tate Britain, London

Selected group exhibitions

2007   *Art Concept*, Paris
2006   *Being in Brussels*, Argos, Brussels
       Just in time, Stedelijk Museum, Amsterdam
2004   *Revenge of romance*, Temporary
       Contemporary, London
       Three to the power of three, Cine Lumière,
       French Institute, London

Exhibited work

6 things we couldn't do, but can do now 2004
Performance and installation
Mixed media
Courtesy the artists

Karin Ruggaber

Born in Germany, 1969
Lives and works in London

| 1996–8 | MFA Sculpture, Slade School of Fine Art, London |
| 1993–6 | BA Hons Fine Art, Chelsea College of Art and Design, London |

Selected solo exhibitions

2005	*Mega-süper military style*, greengrassi, London
2003	*US work and men's shirts*, greengrassi, London
2002	*Rene Daniels and Karin Ruggaber*, Bloomberg SPACE, London

Selected group exhibitions

2006	*How to Improve the World, 60 years of British Art,* Arts Council Collection, Hayward Gallery, London
2005	*The Way We Work Now*, Camden Arts Centre, London
2004	*Ideal Standard*, Dexia Art Centre, Brussels

Exhibited work
Listed as installed from left to right

Relief #20 2006
Plaster
76 × 53 × 2 cm

Relief #15 2006
Concrete, bark, cotton and plaster
85 × 62 × 5 cm

Scarf #2 2005
Cotton and nylon
19 × 15 × 1 cm

Relief #17 2006
Concrete, plaster, wool, tweed and cotton
32 × 29 × 8 cm

Relief #12 2006
Concrete, plaster, wood, silk, felt and tweed
45 × 50 × 4 cm

Wall hanging #1 2006
Wool, tweed, linen, cotton and acrylic
80 × 105 × 5 cm

Relief #19 2006
Plaster, pigment and wool
48 × 44 × 2 cm

Relief #13 2006
Concrete, plaster, wool and tweed
40 × 80 × 5 cm

Scarf #1 2006
Silk and cotton
23 × 13 × 3 cm

Relief #6 2006
Concrete, plaster, bark, cotton and tweed
120 × 107 × 2.5 cm

Relief #2 2005
Concrete, plaster, wood, silk, cotton, wool and tweed
78 × 38 × 4 cm

Relief #18 2006
Plaster and pigment
32 × 49 × 1.5 cm

Wall hanging #2 2006
Cotton, wool, tweed, linen and acrylic
95 × 110 × 5 cm

Relief #7 2005
Concrete, plaster, wood, silk, cotton, wool and tweed
78 × 38 × 4 cm

All works courtesy the artist and greengrassi, London

Raqib Shaw

Born in India, 1974
Lives and works in London

2001–2	MA Fine Art, Central Saint Martins College of Art and Design, London
1998– 2001	BA Fine Art, Central Saint Martins College of Art and Design, London

Selected solo exhibitions

2006	*Raqib Shaw: Garden of Earthly Delights*, Museum of Contemporary Art, Miami Art Now, Tate Britain, London
2005	*Raqib Shaw: Garden of Earthly Delights*, Deitch Projects, New York
2004	*Raqib Shaw: Garden of Earthly Delights*, Victoria Miró Gallery, London

Selected group exhibitions

2006	*Passion for Paint*, National Gallery, London *Around the World in Eighty Days*, Institute of Contemporary Arts, London *6th Gwangju Biennale*, Gwangju *Without Boundary: Seventeen Ways of Looking*, Museum of Modern Art, New York

Exhibited work

Garden of Earthly Delights X 2005
Synthetic polymer paint, glitter, stones, crystals, rhinestones, and gems on board, three panels
244 × 451 cm
Collection of the Museum of Modern Art, New York. Gift of Adam Sender and George Lindemann Jr., 2005

Altarpiece 2006
Industrial paint, glitter and crystal
194 × 240 cm
Courtesy the artist

Anne 2006
Industrial paint, glitter and crystal
87 × 109 cm
Courtesy the artist

Henry VIII 2006
Industrial paint, glitter and crystal
152.5 × 91.7 cm
Courtesy the artist

Jane 2006
Industrial paint, glitter and crystal
92 × 58 cm
Courtesy the artist

Maquette 2006
Polyurethane, epoxy resin and gemstones
40 × 72 × 50 cm
Courtesy the artist

Reflections I 2006
Industrial paint, glitter and crystal
74.7 × 105.3 cm
Courtesy the artist and Deitch Projects, New York

Reflections II 2006
Industrial paint, glitter and crystal
74.7 × 105.3 cm
Courtesy the artist and Deitch Projects, New York

Reflections III 2006
Industrial paint, glitter and crystal
74.7 × 105.3 cm
Courtesy the artist and Deitch Projects, New York

Jamie Shovlin

Born in Leicester, 1978
Lives and works in London

2001–3　MA Painting, Royal College of Art, London
1998–　BA Hons Fine Art Painting, Loughborough
2001　University School of Art & Design

Selected solo exhibitions

2007　*A Dream Deferred*, Haunch of Venison,
　　　London
　　　Aggregate, ArtSway, Sway; City Gallery,
　　　Leicester; Talbot Rice Gallery, Edinburgh
　　　and Hatton Gallery, Newcastle
2006　*Lustfaust: A Folk Anthology*, Freight &
　　　Volume, New York
　　　In Search of Perfect Harmony, Art Now,
　　　Tate Britain, London
2005　*Fontana Modern Masters*, Riflemaker,
　　　London

Selected group exhibitions

2007　*Elephant Cemetery*, Artist's Space,
　　　New York
2006　*Naturalia*, Unosunove, Rome
　　　Beck's Futures, Institute of Contemporary
　　　Arts, London and tour
2005　*After the Fact*, Tullie House Museum,
　　　Carlisle
2004　*Galleon & Other Stories*, Saatchi Gallery,
　　　London

Exhibited work

In Search of Perfect Harmony 2003–6

Crayola Colour Chart
120 wax crayons, inkjet prints, wax crayon and
pencil on paper, archive frame
62 × 62 cm

In Search of Perfect Harmony
30 archive drop-front boxes each containing
a wax crayon frottage and inkjet print on
Somerset Velvet paper
Dimensions variable

The Twitcher 2004–6

Rear Garden of 37 Charles Drive (Bird's Eye View)
Watercolour and pencil on paper, entomology pins
and case
61 × 51 cm

The Birds in her Garden
22 entomology cases each containing a coloured
drawing, index card, book page and entomology pins
Dimensions variable

The Twitcher (Narrative Track)
Two synchronised compact discs played through
four speakers
Dimensions variable

Untitled
DVD and 120 35 mm slides projected onto either side
of an upturned paving slab, DVD projector and 35 mm
slide projector
DVD, 3 min 36 sec

Untitled
Photograph of the artist's mother
Edition of 5
16 × 20 cm

The Origin of Species 2005–6

*The Origin of Species (Sir Thomas Picton School,
Haverfordwest & Emma Bryant)*
Permanent marker, pen and pencil on two used copies
of Charles Darwin's *Origin of Species*, archival mount
board, etching ink, origin stamp
122 × 81.7 cm

*The Origin of Species (University of Brighton &
J. Allan Morton)*
Permanent marker, pen and pencil on two used copies
of Charles Darwin's *Origin of Species*, archival mount
board, etching ink, origin stamp
122 × 81.7 cm

*The Origin of Species (University of Exeter &
Leonard Fellows)*
Permanent marker, pen and pencil on two used copies
of Charles Darwin's *Origin of Species*, archival
mountboard, etching ink, origin stamp
122 × 81.7 cm

All works courtesy the artist and Riflemaker, London

Melanie Smith

Born in Poole, 1965
Lives and works in Mexico City

1984–8   University of Reading

Selected solo exhibitions

2007   *Parres*, in colaboration with Rafael Ortega,
        Galeria OMR, Mexico City
2006   *Spiral City and other Vicarious Pleasures*,
        MUCA Campus, Mexico City
2005   Galerie Peter Kilchmann, Zurich
2004   Museum of Contemporary Art, San Diego

Selected group exhibitions

2007   *The Age of Discrepancies, Art and Visual
        Culture in Mexico 1968–1997*, Museo de
        Ciencias y Artes Campus Universitario,
        Mexico City
2006   *Pasion/Provocation – fotografia & video
        en la Coleccion de Teofilo Cohen*, Centro
        de la Imagen, Mexico City
2005   *Beyond Delirious / Indeterminate States*,
        Cisneros Fontanals Art Foundation, Miami

Rafael Ortega

Born in Mexico City, 1965
Lives and works in Mexico City

Since 1989 Ortega has worked as Director of Photography
on more than forty fiction and documentary productions.
He has collaborated regularly with artists of his
generation since 1994, including Francis Alÿs, João
Penalva, Damián Ortega and Abraham Cruzvillegas.

Exhibited work: Melanie Smith with Rafael Ortega

Parres – Trilogy 2004–6

Parres I 2004
4 min 20 sec

Parres II 2004
3 min 42 sec

Parres III 2006
4 min 20 sec

All works film transferred to DVD and
Dimensions variable

All works courtesy the artists, Galería OMR, Mexico
and Galerie Peter Kilchmann, Switzerland.

Stephen Sutcliffe

Born in 1968
Lives and works in Glasgow

Selected solo exhibitions

2005   *Tart Contemporary*, San Francisco
2003   *Project Space*, Tramway, Glasgow

Selected group exhibitions

2005   Art Now Lightbox, Tate Britain, London
2004   *Pass the Time of Day*, Gasworks, London
        and tour
2003   *Zenomap*, Scottish Pavilion, Venice
        Biennale, Venice
        Electric Earth: Film and Video from Britain,
        State Russian Museum, St Petersburg

Exhibited work

Come to the Edge 2003
DVD, 1 min 49 sec

Transformations 2005
DVD, 1 min 56 sec

All works courtesy the artist

Joanne Tatham

Born in 1971
Lives and works in Glasgow

2000–4   Ph.D., Leeds University
1993–5   MFA Fine Art, Glasgow School of Art
1990–3   BA Fine Art, Duncan of Jordanstone
          College of Art, Dundee

Tom O'Sullivan

Born in 1967
Lives and works in Glasgow

1992–4   MFA Fine Art, Glasgow School of Art
1987–91   BA Fine Art, Leeds University

Selected solo exhibitions

2007   *A fee to avoid our expenses*, The Modern
        Institute / Toby Webster Ltd, Glasgow
2006   *Rhetoric Works & Vanity Works & Other
        Work*, Newhailes, Musselburgh, Edinburgh
        Three Lean Meanings, 'Scotland & Venice'
        touring to Pittenweem Arts Festival, Fife
2005   *Is this what brings things into focus?*,
        Sutton Lane, London
        Oh We Will, We Will, Will We, Studio
        Voltaire, London
2004   *That is the way, it is, it is, that is*, Sutton Lane,
        London
2003   *Thing Thingamajig and Other Things*,
        Kunsthaus Glarus, Switzerland
2001   *HK*, Tramway, Glasgow

Selected group exhibitions

2007   *Half Square, Half Crazy*, Villa Arson, Nice
2006   *Try Again. Fail Again. Fail Better.*,
        Momentum 2006, Nordic Festival
        of Contemporary Art, Moss, Norway
2005   *Scotland & Venice: Selective Memory*,
        51st Venice Biennale
        Art Sheffield 05: Spectator T, Sheffield
        Contemporary Art Forum, Sheffield
2004   *Frieze Projects*, Frieze Art Fair, London
        Hit and Run, platform Garanti, Istanbul
2003   *Zenomap*, 50th Venice Biennale
2002   *The Best Book About Pessimism I Ever Read*,
        Kunstverein Braunschweig, Germany
        *My Head is on Fire but My Heart is Full of
        Love*, Charlottenborg Museum, Copenhagen
2001   *Berlin Biennale 2*, Kunstwerke, Berlin

Exhibited work

Think, Think Thingamajig; what do you represent?
2006
Mixed media – Performance
Courtesy the artists

David Thorpe

Born in London, 1972
Lives and works in London

1996–8   MA Fine Art, Goldsmiths College,
University of London
1991–4   BA Hons Fine Art, Humberside University,
England

Selected solo exhibitions

2007   *The Defeated Life Restored*, Camden Arts
Centre, London
2006   *The Defeated Life Restored*, Kunsthaus
Glarus, Museum Kurhaus Kleve, Kleve
2005   Maureen Paley, London
303 Gallery, New York
2004   *The Colonist*, Meyer Riegger Galerie,
Karlsruhe
The Colonist, Art Now, Tate Britain, London
2003   Taro Nasu Gallery, Tokyo
2002   Maureen Paley, London
1999   Maureen Paley, London

Selected group exhibitions

2006   *Sleep of Ulro*, A Foundation, Liverpool,
curated by Goshka Macuga
Toutes Compositions Florales, Counter
Gallery, London
2005   *Ideal Worlds: New Romanticism in
Contemporary Art*, Schirn Kunsthalle,
Frankfurt
British Art Show 6, Hayward Gallery
national touring exhibition
2004   *Into My World*, The Aldrich Contemporary
Art Museum, Ridgefield
Edge of the Real – A Painting Show,
Whitechapel Art Gallery, London

Exhibited work

A Confederacy of Seekers 2004
Mixed media collage
62 × 41 cm
Courtesy the artist, Meyer Riegger Galerie, Karlsruhe,
and Maureen Paley, London

A Meeting of Friends 2004
Mixed media sculpture
14 × 12 × 10 cm
Courtesy Pojo and Anita Zabludowicz Collection

Eternity and Resistance 2004
Plaster, leather
182 × 597 cm
Courtesy Goetz Collection, Munich

*History is nothing, the world is nothing, our love can
make us clean* 2004
Mixed media collage
56 × 112 cm
Courtesy Goetz Collection, Munich

The Axe Cuts the Root 2004
Mixed media
12 × 11.2 × 38 cm
Courtesy the artist, Meyer Riegger Galerie, Karlsruhe,
and Maureen Paley, London

The Axe Laid on the Root 2004
Mixed media collage
63 × 90 cm
Courtesy Private Collection, Cologne

The Colonist 2004
Mixed media collage
82.9 × 40 cm
Courtesy Goetz Collection, Munich

The Hidden Language 2004
Mixed media collage
42 × 146 cm
Collection Michael Heins, Herzogenrath, Germany

The Protecting Army I 2004
Wood, glass
232 × 194.7 cm
Courtesy Goetz Collection, Munich

The Protecting Army II 2004
Wood, glass
205 × 223 cm
Courtesy the artist, Meyer Riegger Galerie, Karlsruhe,
and Maureen Paley, London

David Thorpe continued:

The Protecting Army III 2004
Wood, glass
22.3 × 20.5 cm
Courtesy Goetz Collection, Munich

The Protecting Army IV 2004
Wood, glass
232 × 406 cm
Courtesy the artist, Meyer Riegger Galerie, Karlsruhe,
and Maureen Paley, London

The Protecting Army V 2004
Wood, glass
23 × 21 cm
Courtesy the artist, Meyer Riegger Galerie, Karlsruhe,
and Maureen Paley, London

The White Brotherhood, 2004
Glass, wood and found objects
138 × 107 × 930 cm
Courtesy Goetz Collection, Munich

Untitled (Armoured Bud) 2004
Watercolour and pencil on paper
56 × 37 cm
Courtesy Goetz Collection, Munich

Untitled (Green Spears) 2004
Plaster, leather
182 × 330 cm
Courtesy Goetz Collection, Munich

Untitled (Star Petals) 2004
Watercolour and pencil on paper
62 × 46 cm
Courtesy Private Collection, Herzogenrath

Untitled (Yellow Barrier) 2004
Acrylic and transparent foil on brown paper
565 × 518 cm
Courtesy Goetz Collection, Munich

Sue Tompkins

Born in 1971
Lives and works in Glasgow

Selected solo exhibitions

2007   Diana Stigter Gallery, Amsterdam
        The Showroom, London
2006   *Transfer* with Hayley Tompkins,
        Spike Island, Bristol
        Café design commission with architects
        Caruso St John with Hayley Tompkins,
        Spike Island, Bristol
        Solo, The Modern Institute / Toby Webster
        Ltd, Glasgow
2005   *Hayley Tompkins and Sue Tompkins*,
        Andrew Kreps Gallery, New York
        When it broke, ArtForum Berlin,
        Galerie Giti Nourbakhsch, Berlin
        Elephants Galore, Live performance,
        Selective Memory opening, Scottish
        Pavillion, Venice Biennale

Selected group exhibitions

2007   *Learn To Read*, Tate Modern, London
2006   *Try Again. Fail Again. Fail Better*,
        4th Nordic Festival of Contemporary Art,
        Moss
        Attitudes, Atle Gerhardsen Gallery, Berlin
        Satellites, Tanya Bonakdar Gallery,
        New York
        Beck's Futures, ICA, London; CCA off-site,
        Glasgow; Arnolfini off-site, Bristol

Exhibited work

Grease 2006
Performance
Courtesy the artist

Emily Wardill

Born in 1977
Lives and works in London

Emily Wardill is part of the Collective Boxing Club
working from Limehouse Town Hall and co-organises
the performance, live music and screening event
Itchy Park.

Selected solo exhibitions

2006   *Basking in what feels like 'an ocean of grace',*
        I soon realise that I'm not looking at it but
        rather that I AM it, recognising myself,
        Fortescue Avenue, London
2005   *The Reader's Wife*, Fortescue Avenue,
        London

Selected group exhibitions

2007   *Pastoral*, Whitechapel Art Gallery, London
        Kinomuseum, curated by Ian White
        and Emily Pethick, Oberhausen Short Film
        Festival
2006   Art Now Lightbox, Tate Britain, London
2005   *High Risk Painting*, Northern Gallery for
        Contemporary Art, Sunderland
2004   *Romantic Detachment*, P.S.1 Contemporary
        Art Center, New York
2004   *Residency,* Grizedale Arts, Lake District

Exhibited work

Born Winged Animals and Honey Gatherers of the Soul
2005
16 mm film with sound transferred onto DVD, 9 min
Courtesy the artist and Jonathan Viner/Fortescue
Avenue. Supported by Arts Council England.

Martin Westwood

Born in Sheffield, 1969
Lives and works in London

1992–4   MA Fine Art, Royal College of Art, London
1988–92 BA Hons Fine Art, Chelsea College of Art
         and Design, London

Selected solo exhibitions

2007   The Approach, London
2006   Art Statements, Art 37 Basel
2005   *fade held*, Art Now, Tate Britain, London
2004   *Angelus Novus*, Collective Gallery,
       Edinburgh
2003   *Hard Pressed Flowers*, The Approach,
       London

Selected group exhibitions

2005   *CUT*, The Approach, London
2004   *Reflections*, Artuaca Kunsterfgoed Festival,
       Tongeren
       Wider Than The Sky, 117 Commercial
       Street, London
       Concert in the Egg, The Ship, London
2003   *Dirty Pictures*, The Approach, London

Exhibited work

Fade 2005
106 parts stainless steel
Dimensions variable

Fold 2005
Acrylic on 4 walls
244 × 122 cm

Held 2005
Lithographic print, map pins on pin board in
walnut frame (2 parts)
Dimensions variable

Hold 2005
Upholstered table, shredded office stationery,
photocopy, glass, map pins, pen and stone
91.5 × 152.5 cm

Return 2005
Shredded lithographic prints on two papier-mâché
balloons and twine
40 × 40 × 55 cm

Thread 2005
Acrylic on 5 walls
240 × 122 cm

Turn 2005
4 wooden spiral staircases
122 × 122 × 93 cm

All works courtesy the artist and The Approach,
London

Ian White

Born in Dagenham, 1971
Lives and works in London

2001–	Adjunct Film Curator, Whitechapel Art
present	Gallery, London
2000–1	Curator, Lux Cinema, London

Selected exhibitions

2005	*Treehugger: Now/Romantic/Nature*, Group exhibition, Showroom MAMA, Rotterdam
2004	*6 things we couldn't do, but can do now*, Art Now, Tate Britain, London
2003	*The Neon Gainsborough*, Neon Gallery, London
2002	*FAG* with Jimmy Robert and Emma Hedditch, Cubitt, London

Selected curatorial projects

2007	*Kinomuseum*, Internationale Kurzfilmtage Oberhausen
2006–7	*The Secret Public: The Last Days of the British Underground 1978–1988*, Associate Curator, Kunstverein Munich & Institute of Contemporary Art, London
2005–6	The Artists' Cinema, Co-ordinator, Frieze Art Fair, London
2005	*Der Geist ist Ein Wasserfall*, Klaus Weber monographic exhibition, Showroom MAMA, Rotterdam
2004	*3 to the Power of 3*, Cine Lumière, Institut Francais, London

Exhibited work

6 things we couldn't do, but can do now 2004
Performance and installation
Mixed media
Courtesy the artists

Acknowledgements
The curators would like to thank all the artists
who have participated in Art Now, their galleries,
and all the lenders to the exhibition

Photographic credits
Tate Photography: M. Heathcote, J. Fernandes,
D. Lambert, R. Tidnam & S. Drake
Jananne Al-Ani: Effie Paleologou (*Muse*),
Bevis Bowden (installation views)
Sheila Burnett
Kate Davis: The Estate of Jacob Epstein/Tate
(*Your body is a battleground still*)
Karin Ruggaber: Michael Franke
Martin Westwood & Inventory: FXP Photography,
London

All other images are courtesy the artists
and their galleries